Christ and

Wilhelm Kelber

Christ and the Son of Man

Floris Books

Translated by Hildegard Stossel
Edited by Jon Madsen

First published in 1967 under the title
Der Menschensohn by Verlag Urachhaus, Stuttgart
First published in English in 1997 by Floris Books

British Library CIP Data available

ISBN 0-86315-251-1

Printed in Great Britain
by Redwood Books, Wilts

Contents

Acknowledgments

The publisher would like to acknowledge the work of Hildegard Stossel in bringing this book, first published in German thirty years ago, to an English-speaking audience.

Unless otherwise marked, quotations from the New Testament are from the rendering by Jon Madsen (published by Floris Books). Scriptural passages marled RSV are from the Revised Standard Version, and those marked REB are from the Revised English Bible.

Preface

Again and again during the last seventy years theological research has investigated what might be meant by 'the Son of Man,' a term used in the gospels to describe the Christ. Whatever these methods of research could find has been collected and discovered. The most important discoveries were: that 'Son of Man' is only ever used to describe Christ by Christ himself; that the first time this self-designation is heard is in a solemn hour in the presence of the disciples only; that the disciples are told not to talk about it until the day of Resurrection; that the fact that the Christ is the Son of Man is therefore protected, secret knowledge for the disciples; that this designation is found earlier, since the time of the prophet Daniel, in some canonical and apocryphal books of the Old Testament; and finally, that in the *Book of Enoch,* it takes on the character of the central part of an esoteric wisdom that was kept in closed circles of late Judaism.

Here let us unequivocally express our appreciation of all the work that has been done. The fact that there are limitations to the result of this labour is a consequence of the mind-set of modern scientism which refuses to include an objective spiritual world within its range of vision. So the question as to whether the prophets' visions of the Son of Man could possibly be based on an actual Being was never asked; but this means that the question of the *truth* of all this has never been asked. And so the Son of Man of late Judaism was regarded as a 'religious conception,' albeit 'one of the most sublime ever to have arisen in the history of religion,' to quote R. Otto.

In the New Testament this designation was regarded as an 'honorary title' bestowed upon the Christ (O. Cullmann). In addition, the term Son of Man had, from the very beginning (H. Lietzmann) been understood purely grammatically rather than imaginatively as a pictorial word; and thereby its significance was missed.

The starting point of the present work was a concrete question: Does a being — the Son of Man — exist, who can be distinguished from the being of the Christ in a similar way as the Logos can be distinguished from the man Jesus? Do the Christ's 'Son of Man' words provide the outline of such a being? How does the image that may thus emerge relate to the Son of Man of the Jewish prophets?

The first chapter provides an investigative framework. If it is true that knowledge of the Son of Man belongs to the esoteric body of knowledge of the disciples, can this be confirmed by the whole way in which this designation is used in the gospels? If so, then it is clear from the outset that we are dealing neither with an abstract 'title' nor a pious 'conception' but with a reality in the Christ's nature.

In the second chapter all statements about the Son of Man found in the New Testament are grouped together and examined. As far as possible, we have avoided drawing conclusions other than those arising immediately out of the words themselves. It was the intention to let an image of the Son of Man emerge from the totality of the statements themselves. Obvious conclusions arising from the statements have been kept in the form of questions.

The Son of Man motifs of the Old Testament books are

presented in the third chapter. They differ from those in the gospels in two respects. Firstly, the Son of Man is beheld here as a supersensory being; and then there is also a kind of doctrine of the Son of Man, especially in the *Book of Enoch.* We examine how the Son of Man of these Jewish prophecies and apocalypses, perceived from outside and presented in teachings, relates to the being of whom the Christ speaks. Here, too, we attempt to let the various elements which correspond to and supplement each other build up the essence of an image.

The fourth chapter, finally, sets out what is contained in Rudolf Steiner's Anthroposophy about the 'Adam soul' on the one hand, and the Son of Man on the other. On closer examination, it appears that the two groups of statements belong together; and the images of the Son of Man, as they arise out of both the Christian and the Jewish traditions, complement each other to a wonderful wholeness. Unanswered questions from previous chapters can be resolved fully.

Our traditional image of the Christ undergoes considerable change when we begin to grasp the nature of the being of the Son of Man. Not, however, by a deviation from Christian revelation, but rather by the cognitive insight that the words of Christ about the Son of Man are wholly and literally true.

It should be noted that the Christ being and the death on Golgotha are presented here under the particular aspect of the Son of Man, as the subject of this book demands. This leads to a certain onesidedness, because other sides of anthroposophical Christology could not be considered to the same extent and have only been included where necessary to avoid misunderstandings.

With the exception of some general remarks, no

attempt has been made to deal with methods and results of the work undertaken so far by theology. Interested readers who want to scrutinize the spiritual-scientific method of this book, will be able to see how the anthroposophical background makes it possible to cross the limiting threshold of cognition before which today's abstract philological research stops.

Without belief in the Son of Man none of the words about him make sense. The work presented here is about establishing this belief.

The author is indebted to Rudolf Frieling, Robert Goebel, Eberhard Kurras, Rudolf Meyer, Reinhard Wagner and Kurt von Wistinghausen for their critical examination of the manuscript. However, the author alone is responsible for the contents.

1. More than another name for Jesus Christ

The Son of Man in the New Testament

'Son of Man' is the most significant and enigmatic formula in the New Testament. In Greek it consists of four words: *ho huios tou anthropou,* the son of the human being. The use of two articles, which in Greek is uncommon, elevates it beyond everyday language. And in the Greek genitive, in its masculine form, there still lives the sound of something of the fundamental and original connection between people and objects. With the aid of simple genitives the genealogical tree of Jesus is traced back to 'Adam of God' (Luke 3:23–38).

Furthermore, this formula (that is, Son of Man) is only ever used in the gospels by Christ himself, and then only to describe himself, so that it literally is a 'word of God,' a sequence of words that only ever issues from the mouth of a god, through which a god says something about himself.

Theologians might claim that wherever Christ speaks of himself as Son of Man, he could equally well say 'I.' This view is based on the fact that one and the same pronouncement can be expressed in the first person as well as through the Son of Man formula. However, it is wrong to conclude that there is nothing very special about statements made in the Son of Man form, that, indeed, they are always interchangeable with sayings in the first person. What is correct is that in the sayings of Christ, Son of Man occupies the same rank as the self-designation 'I.' The remarkable fact that nobody else ever called Christ the Son of Man while he lived on earth, shows that this was no more possible than saying 'I' to another person. The Christ's ego-consciousness included the Son of Man. But Christ's ability to speak of this Son of Man in the third person raises the question whether there was an 'I' contained in his being, perhaps the Logos, which, however, is not to be equated with the Son of Man. We shall have to concern ourselves with this question.

In order to fathom the mystery of the Son of Man we shall first have to examine where, under what circumstances and in which context Christ's self-designation occurs in the gospels. According to St John's Gospel, the Christ spoke seven I-am-words in the emphatic form, *ego eimi,* the special significance of which was first recognized by Friedrich Rittelmeyer. Although statements made in the first person can, by their content, not strictly be distinguished from those in the Son of Man form, an examination of the Son of Man sayings by themselves is still the best way to come to grips with the significance of this term.

The 'Son of Man' formula appears eighty-one times in the gospels: thirty times in Matthew, thirteen times in Mark, twenty-six times in Luke and twelve times in John. Of course, these figures tell us no more than that 'the Son of Man' is among the fundamental concepts of all four gospels and that it is most frequently found with Matthew — the gospel writer with the closest ties to the Jewish tradition — and with Luke, the pupil of Paul. If one takes account of passages in the various gospels with parallel content, and if one also regards as parallel those passages that have similar content albeit with minor variations, one is left with approximately forty statements in Son of Man form, enriching this concept with various images.

Before grouping and explaining the contents of the Christ's statements delivered in Son of Man form, we can gain fundamental insights by examining the settings for these sayings and the persons to whom they were addressed. The first three gospels clearly identify the occasion when Christ first calls himself Son of Man, though the formula appears in the gospels earlier. It is the scene of recognition at Caesarea Philippi (Matt.16:13ff, Mark 8:27ff, Luke 9:18ff).* This is where Peter first recognizes Jesus of Nazareth as the Messiah (Greek: *Christos).* Recognized, Jesus exhorts the disciples to keep silent about the event and continues to speak about himself, not as Messiah but as Son of Man. And what he says is in such sharp contrast to the ideas commonly held about the expected Messiah, that these ideas, which also live in Peter, must be rejected in the strongest terms. What the disciples are confronted with is Christ's self-revelation which they clearly cannot yet grasp, and for which even Peter's insight is not yet sufficient. This insight was a superhuman achievement and is acknowledged by Christ with high praise:

> Blessed are you, Simon, son of Jona; you have not received this revelation from the world of the senses but from the world of my Father in the heavens (Matt.16:17).

* See Oscar Cullmann, *Die Christologie des Neuen Testaments,* Chapter 2.

But immediately afterwards, when it becomes clear that Peter's ideas of the Messiah are quite different from those which Christ at that moment had wanted to inspire in the disciples in relation to the Son of Man the dreadful words follow:

> Leave me, power of Satan. Your aim is to alienate me from my purpose. You are no longer thinking heavenly thoughts; now you are only thinking as earthly Man. (Matt.16:23).

We would not be doing justice to the event of Caesarea Philippi, if we were to consider it on the level of ordinary processes of thought and emotion, and understand Christ's replies simply as high praise and sharp rebuke. Rather, what we are dealing with here is an initiation process, in the course of which Peter, representing the disciples, in short succession has to ascend two stages of consciousness. But the Adversary intervenes, as can easily happen on the paths of higher levels of perception. We may take the form of address the Christ uses in his rebuke, quite literally. He banishes Satan who wants to prevent Peter's consciousness from reaching imminently the level that must be attained if the Son of Man is to be understood.

In all three synoptic gospels the scene at Caesarea Philippi is followed immediately by the Transfiguration which makes great demands on the capacity for supersensory perception of the three disciples Peter, James and John. They are to behold the Christ in his divine spirit form between the spirits of Moses and Elijah. The composition of the three gospels characterizes the dramatic happening of Caesarea Philippi that went before, as a preparation and preliminary stage of the Transfiguration. This too, speaks for the notion that with the revelation of the secret of the Son of Man, the spiritual guidance of the disciples assumes the character of an initiation. And so we also understand in a deeper sense the urgent demand for silence which Christ imposes on the disciples. Knowledge of the Son of Man is initiation knowledge and is not to be spread about like ordinary knowledge acquired through the intellect. Knowledge of the Son of Man is esoteric knowledge which the disciples carry with them to the final drama in the Christ's earthly life.

Checking the gospels for frequency of the term Son of Man, we find that it occurs nine times in Matthew, twice in Mark and three times in Luke, *before* the account of the event of Caesarea Philippi. In John, where this event is not mentioned, the Christ's self-designation appears at least twice (1:51; 3:13) so early on that it must have been before this first revelation was made to the disciples. Theological research, having recognized that Christ's revelation of himself as the Son of Man began at Caesarea Philippi, assumes correctly that the gospel writers, who of course all wrote *after* the events they report, also use the self-designation Son of Man in Christ's speeches in scenes that either occurred chronologically before Peter's confession, or which at any rate are described by them earlier. The gospels show clearly enough that their compositions are dictated by principles other than historical ones, according to which events would have to be described in the order in which they took place. This also applies to the Christ's statements in Son of Man form. We find the same saying recorded once before and once after the happening of Caesarea Philippi. Our examination will show that it makes sense even before the event.

For some of the places where the Son of Man motif occurs early, an alternative explanation is also possible. It is suggested by the first two passages in John's Gospel. There Christ reveals himself as Son of Man to two very special personalities, Nathanael and Nicodemus.

Nathanael and Nicodemus

Nathanael is that enigmatic personality who only appears in the first and last chapter of John's Gospel and in no other book of the New Testament. He meets Christ immediately after the first three disciples have been called and at once recognizes him as the Son of God, long before Peter has this insight. However, he is not called to the circle of disciples like the fishermen from the Sea of Galilee.* He receives a promise concerning his future spiritual perception. A man, then, who does not have to take on the apostolic task of proclaiming and spreading Christianity, but who is shown a way to develop his supersensory powers of perception. This may well be the reason why he now disappears from the gospels' field of vision. But at the last appearance of the Risen One 'at the sea near Tiberias,' he is mentioned once more as one of the seven disciples who are granted this vision (John 21:2). Five of these disciples are named. And their names indicate the character of the group. There are the three disciples who awoke to supersensory perception at the Transfiguration. Then there is Thomas who has overcome his doubts, the first 'intellectual' to be healed. And there is Nathanael. A group of advanced seekers of insight whose eyes had been opened for this last supersensory

* Attempts have been made to identify Nathanael with Bartholomew, in order to accommodate him among the twelve disciples. It has to be acknowledged, though, that there is a whole series of personalities who, despite their close relationship to Christ, do not belong to the circle of the twelve.

event of fishing and taking bread and fish. One could perhaps say that Nathanael accompanied the ways of Christ to the end, if not on the roads of the Holy Land, then nevertheless in the spirit.

Who was this Nathanael? He is singled out in the first chapter of John's Gospel by means which, Rudolf Steiner was able to interpret. The fact that Christ saw Nathanael 'under the fig tree' opened his eyes to the nature of the man, for 'fig tree' is the mystery term for path to supersensory knowledge still valid at that time. Christ saw Nathanael as he was immersed in the realm of the spirit. That convinced this initiate. The word that Christ uses to describe Nathanael is also taken from mystery language: 'He really has reached the stage of an Israelite in whom there is no untruth' (John 1:47). In the old mysteries the name of the nation was a symbol for the fifth degree of initiation, in which the initiate grows beyond his individual nature and becomes the spiritual bearer of spirit and destiny of his people.* Nathanael was the first to recognize Christ as the Son of God, and he revealed himself to Nathanael as the Son of Man, before Peter was deemed worthy.

Nicodemus, too, is named only in the Gospel of St John; in the very beginning, in the third chapter, and again towards the end (19:39). And in between once more, in the seventh chapter. Nicodemus we can also describe as a follower but not a disciple of the Christ. He receives instruction regarding the paths that lead to 'beholding the kingdom of God' (3:3). He, too, seeks such paths. His stage of progress is also here indicated by a mystery term. He comes to the Christ 'by night.'

* See Emil Bock, *The Three Years,* p.163ff.

According to Rudolf Steiner's indications this means that he comes to the Christ in an out-of-body condition during sleep; that is to say, he can keep his consciousness alert while spiritually outside his body. If this coming 'by night' were intended merely to indicate the time of the visit, it would at most have been mentioned only here, where this coming is reported (3:2); indeed, because of its insignificance it would probably not have been recorded at all. But when several manuscripts in the seventh chapter append 'he that came to Jesus by night' (7:50) to the name Nicodemus we see that Nicodemus is characterized as one who was able to come by night. The same applies later (19:39). He is not named without this characterization which testifies that Nicodemus has reached the stage of 'continuing consciousness.'

He did not follow Christ in a physical sense. He kept his position as a member of the Sanhedrin, the highest Council of the Jews. In his capacity as a man of influence, he once defended the Christ at a meeting of the Council and came under suspicion that 'he, too, is of Galilee,' in other words a follower of the Christ (7:52). And at the last, when the body of Christ hangs deserted on the cross, the disciples having failed him, it is Nicodemus who is present with Joseph of Arimathea. In the evening they take the body from the cross and lay it in the tomb. Nathanael was one of the seven disciples who were granted the last meeting with the Risen One in the realm of the spirit. Nicodemus was one of the two who cared for the sacred body — a service which had to be performed on the Christ's body at the genesis of the sacrament of the altar. Nicodemus is the other spiritual pupil to whom the Christ revealed himself as the Son of Man, *before* he revealed himself to the disciples. We must leave open whether these two initiates were already familiar with the nature of the symbol 'Son of Man' through a tradition which we shall yet get to know, or whether, on the basis of their spiritual development, Christ deemed them worthy and capable of understanding what it meant if he described himself to them as Son of Man.

Zacchaeus

In this connection it seems appropriate to include a passage of Luke's Gospel (19:1–10). The fact that Christ also speaks before Zacchaeus, the tax-collector, of himself as the Son of Man, although happening after Peter's confession, also breaks the rule that until the end nobody but the disciples were to know the secret of the Son of Man. Remarkably, Zacchaeus, too, appears in connection with a tree. The Greek text does not use the word for fig tree *(sykē)* here, but *sykomorea,* sycamore, mulberry tree. This is the tree under which Egyptian initiates are portrayed. Certainly, there is also a straightforward meaning if one is content with taking the images of this story at face value: Zacchaeus was short of stature and therefore climbed a tree in order to see Christ better as he passed by. One may also disregard the fact that Christ's looking up into the tree is described with a phrase which elsewhere in the gospels is solemnly translated: 'and he lifted up his eyes.' And finally, one may not wonder why Christ calls this Zacchaeus, of all people, down from the tree in order to visit him in his house. Was it only that he was touched by the keenness of this climber who wanted to see him at any cost? One can conceivably be satisfied with this superficial explanation, but it will not help in penetrating to the true meaning of this passage. Once the key to the symbol 'tree' is grasped, it is not too difficult to understand what is meant here. Zacchaeus probably feels under pressure, insignificant, small because of his despised occupation, that of a tax-collector. He seeks to compensate for it, morally, by giving half of his wealth to the poor. Unjustly collected taxes he restitutes fourfold. He is modest, feels himself to be less than other people, feels unworthy. But this makes him 'a beggar for spirit,' makes him delve into the inner life of the spirit, makes him seek the 'sycamore.' We do not have to decide here whether an Egyptian path of initiation may have found followers also in the Holy Land, in other words, whether 'sycamore' is used in its exact sense or whether this word stands, a little carelessly, for *sykē,* the word we should expect. And we must not be put off by the fact that here it says 'climbing' the tree instead of 'sitting under' the tree because, firstly, the image of the 'little man' requires that he ascend in order to see Christ. And furthermore, the expression 'climbing the tree' is as correct as 'sitting under the tree,' since the 'tree' expresses pictorially that the initiate puts himself into a state where he no longer feels himself to be in his body but within the organism of his growth-forces (etheric body), which extends beyond the physical body and in which the organs of super-sensory perception are developed. So the transition from everyday physical consciousness to a supersensory one can rightly be called an 'ascent.'

Christ 'lifted up his eyes and saw' Zacchaeus in the sycamore; that is equivalent to 'when you were under the fig tree I saw you' (John 1:48). In both cases we are dealing with the supersensory perception of the spirit form of a human being immersed in deep meditation. And we may assume that it was the humility, the guilt-feelings of this man regarded as a sinner, and his highly developed morality which prompted Christ to be his guest. To this seeker of the spirit, too, Christ reveals the secret of his nature, hidden behind the designation 'Son of Man'; and he says words to him which confirm that our characterization of Zacchaeus is correct.* We shall return to the meaning of these words by which the mission of the Son of Man is also described in other gospel passages (pages 35ff).

Perhaps the best-known passage dealing with the Son of Man is to be understood in a similar spirit as the scene with Nathanael, Nicodemus and Zacchaeus. Luke places it after Peter's confession (9:58), Matthew before it (8:20). There Christ says:

> The foxes have their holes and the birds of heaven have their nests, but the Son of Man has nowhere to lay his head.

Here, too, everything depends upon the situation and to whom these words were spoken. Both gospels report Christ's preceding *departure* with his disciples. With Matthew it is the departure away from the big crowd which had gathered after the healing of the many possessed and sick people in Capernaum. Christ arranges for them to cross the lake. But before they can reach the boat a scribe approaches and says: 'Master, I will follow you wherever you go.' With Luke it is the great departure, after Peter's confession and the Transfiguration, for the place of fulfilment, Jerusalem. The Samaritans refuse Christ shelter in one of their villages, and he wanders on

* In Pseudo-Clementine, Peter instals Zacchaeus as his representative in Rome because of 'the beautiful wisdom with which the Lord has entrusted you' (65:2).

with his disciples to another place. There, 'on the way' there was 'one' who spoke the same words to him: 'I will follow you wherever you go.'

Christ's words, then, are his response to the intention of following him. Both persons, the scribe in Matthew and the 'one' in Luke, appear from nowhere, so to speak, remain anonymous and immediately vanished again, without us learning what they might have gone on to do. This would seem to indicate that it never has been the purpose of the gospel merely to 'tell a tale,' although such scenes surely happened. Rather, it appears that the question about following the Christ was asked twice and both times the conditions were stated, using the same formula. In Matthew it is the emotional shock of being confronted with the immense healing power of the Christ which led this man, this scribe, who has only ever known religious *doctrines*, to ask the question, as the Christ is about to depart. As motivation for discipleship, Luke conveys the image of the Christ, homeless on earth and rejected, tracing his course like a star.

Christ gives something like conditions for acceptance, couched in images. He is aware that the would-be followers have *recognized* him, otherwise they would not want to follow him. And the reply he gives is not addressed to naive souls, but to human beings who now want to walk the spiritual paths with him. The 'one' in Luke had just experienced what it means that Christ is without home anywhere. He did not have to be told. He realized that the physical homelessness described so graphically was a realistic parable for the Christ's relationship to the earth. It is not emotional compassion that is being appealed to with the words: 'The Son of Man has nowhere to lay his head'; rather, it is the spiritual courage to renounce earthly security and home and, like the stars, look for a home in heaven. The reply given to the two candidates for discipleship has the same meaning as the one given to the rich youth (Matt.19:16–21):

> If you desire to reach the highest aim *(téleios),* then sell what you possess and give the proceeds to the poor. By doing that you will acquire a treasure in the heavens. And then come and follow me!

Whereas the conversations with Nathanael, Nicodemus and Zacchaeus are conversations with initiates, the scribe in Matthew and the 'one' in Luke receive initial instructions for the initiation path. Inasmuch as these passages in Matthew and Luke may refer to one or several historical events, the question can arise whether in these cases Christ revealed himself as the Awaited One to such human beings as lived in particular expectation of the 'Son of Man,' in the way in which it can be seen especially in the *Book of Enoch.*

Before Caesarea Philippi

The exception to the rule that Son of Man words are spoken *after* Peter's confession, and then only to the disciples, becomes comprehensible in another sense when we consider some further instances. The first three (synoptic) gospels record two characterizations of the Son of Man *before* the event of Caesarea Philippi, which occurred in the presence of scribes and Pharisees.

One of these revelations concerns the healing of sins. It follows the healing of the paralysed man (Matt.9:1–8, Mark 2:1–12 and Luke 5:17–26). The Christ says to the sick man: 'Take courage, my son, your sins are taken from you.' The scribes present are outraged 'in their hearts' at this presumption. Christ reads their hearts before they can speak, and he says:

> The Son of Man has the authority to forgive
> sins on earth.

No argument arises; before it can develop, the drama takes place in the hearts of the scribes. Their idea of justice is the strict justice of God in the sense of the Old Testament. They know nothing of forgiveness of sins, and especially not during life on earth. Nor does their picture of the Messiah include this notion. And now they are being taught about the nature of the Son of Man who is not their Messiah.

Similar circumstances surround the second scene which is found in Matt.12:1–8, Mark 2:23–38 and Luke 6:1–5. The disciples have picked ears of wheat on a Sabbath, to appease their hunger. The Pharisees reproach them: the commandments pertaining to the Sabbath have been broken. And Christ answers:

> The Son of Man is Lord even of the Sabbath.

On their first meeting with the Christ, the Pharisees are to understand that, with the coming of the Son of Man, righteousness according to the Law loses its validity.

What is important in these two scenes is not so much the content of the statements concerning the Son of Man, as the contrast they provide to the view held by the representatives of the religion of the Old Testament. The Son of Man confronts the just and stern God of Judaism as healer and as founder of human freedom from the morality as decreed by the Law. In the synoptic gospels, these passages — sent ahead, as it were — look like a prologue to the Son of Man proclamations. They serve to show up the contrast to the image of the Messiah familiar to the scribes and Pharisees. They form the stumbling-block which now has appeared in all reality.

There are possible explanations for how these 'anachronistic' Son of Man sayings came about. If we are willing to believe that the gospel writers were inspired, we may assume that those two sayings entered the consciousness of the writers in this form, although historically they may have been delivered in the first person. Or perhaps the gospel writers put these sayings into the Son of Man form out of their own consciousness, being able to judge that Christ spoke *as* the Son of Man at the time, even though he may actually have chosen the first person form. In the first case it would have been inspiration, in the second those inspired who shifted this threshold of the Son of Man proclamation for those coming from old religious traditions. Not least in their composition, the gospels have the character of books of instruction and training.

Caiaphas

Finally, let us look at the last person whom Christ speaks to, using the Son of Man formula. It is the High Priest Caiaphas. Christ has been arrested and brought before the assembly of scribes, Pharisees and elders. They ask him if he is the Messiah, the Son of God. And he replies, speaking of the Son of Man (Matt.26:64, Mark 14:62, Luke 22:69). Matthew provides the clearest picture of the event. Previous translations had Christ say: 'You said it. Nevertheless, I tell you ...' (Matt.26:64). The words in question can equally well be translated: 'That is what *you* say.'* Only then does the 'nevertheless' in the next sentence make sense. The Christ's reply does not constitute an affirmation of Caiaphas' question, but a contrast. Christ does not confess to being the Messiah Caiaphas has in mind, but to being the Son of Man. And what he says of him demonstrates clearly what is meant:

> You will see the Son of Man sitting at the right hand of power, coming in the clouds of the heavens.

This does not correspond to the messianic image of Judaism. Rather, it reminds the judges of an old picture from the Book of Daniel. This is the Son of Man as beheld by Daniel in his vision, and of the tradition that reaches to the *Book of Enoch.* Here, in the night to Good Friday and before the Sanhedrin, Christ states publicly what up to this time has been esoteric knowledge of the circle of disciples: he is the Son of Man.

This last self-confession of the Christ as Son of Man is a counterpart to the first time he speaks in this capacity. Then, too, at Caesarea Philippi Peter had addressed him as Messiah (Matt.16:17, see page 15). The power of perception necessary for this had been acknowledged by Christ as inspiration; by his living and walking with Christ, Peter had achieved this: a human being had recognized that after thousands of years, a divine being was on earth again. But it was more difficult to discern than in olden times because it appeared in a human body. However, when it became obvious that false hopes about

* At that time, the expression 'you said it' was not used among the rabbis as simple affirmation; it was, however, current in the sense 'that is what *you* say, not I.'

the Messiah had crept in, the insight won by Peter had to be corrected. The correction consisted in Christ's revelation of himself as the Son of Man, and at once there followed the prophecy:

> The Son of Man must suffer much and be rejected by the elders and the chief priests and the scribes; and he will be killed (Mark 8:31).

And now, as the cock crows at daybreak on Good Friday, Christ stands before these judges as he had foreseen. Now he is required to confess whether he is the Messiah, the Son of God; whether, therefore, the confession of Peter, who is outside in the courtyard — whether this confession at Caesarea Philippi is valid. What was Peter's cognition and confession is turned into an accusation. And Christ makes the same correction as on the previous occasion. As the Son of Man he must suffer death. From the three accounts describing the passing of the death sentence, the impression arises that Christ's confession to being the Son of Man, sitting at the right hand of God and coming with the clouds of heaven, was the decisive factor. The Sanhedrin might have been more willing to tolerate a Messiah as secular liberator. As it was, the ecclesiastic authority of the Sanhedrin was being challenged.

After the Resurrection

At the beginning it was pointed out that one characteristic of the term 'Son of Man' is its exclusive use by Christ for himself; no other person ever called him by that name. This is true of the entire time he walked the earth. Only after his death three, or strictly speaking four, passages are found in the New Testament where this term describing his nature was given to him by others.

First there are the two angels who remind the women in the empty tomb on Easter morning, that Christ foretold his death and Resurrection in a 'Son of Man' speech. (Luke 24:7). The words used by the angels are very similar to a prophecy Christ makes after the healing of the possessed boy (Matt.17:22, Mark 9:31, Luke 9:44). The women recall these words (Luke 24:8). This, too, is one of the significant connections that bind the Son of Man passages to each other. Recalling that prophecy, the women understand the mystery of the empty tomb and the miracle of the Resurrection. Here, then, it is angels who, using his own words, call Christ Son of Man. Later, it is Stephen, the first martyr, who, before being stoned, 'filled with the Holy Spirit, looked up into heaven and saw the light of the revelation of God, and Jesus standing to the right hand of God.' And he said:

> See, the heavens are opened to my beholding. I see the Son of Man at the right hand of God (Acts 7:55f).

In the first instance, it is angels who use this designation for Christ at the empty tomb; now it is a human being in supersensory perception, on facing death. Whether he, too, is thinking of words he once heard spoken by Christ, or whether the vision itself prompts him to choose this term, either way the scene is already set in the spirit realm, and the name applies to the Risen and Ascended One.

The third one is the seer John. In his Revelation, he twice calls the Christ whom he beholds in the spirit world, Son of Man; once in his spirit form standing in the midst of the seven golden lights (1:13), and then at the harvest of the earth as Christ sits on a cloud with the sickle in his hand (14:14). An image that, as we shall see later, is connected with a function of the Son of Man that the Christ has named and which had already been foretold in Jewish prophecy.

Out of the consciousness of angels and seers the Risen Christ is called Son of Man. In each of these, this means a confirmation or fulfilment of Son of Man words previously spoken by Christ: death and Resurrection, sitting at the right hand of God, the office of judge ('harvest of the earth'). Yet the fact that only angels and seers are able to call the Christ by a name he himself used while walking the earth, suggests that 'Son of Man' is the name for a part of the Christ being which eludes everyday consciousness; that human beings will have to develop further before they can come to perceive this aspect of the Christ being. In the Chapter 3 we shall see that the Son of Man had appeared before the spiritual eye of seers for centuries, and that knowledge of him was limited to esoteric circles. Such knowledge of the Son of Man is used in the New Testament in accordance with this tradition.

2. The Son of Man, the Son of God, the Saviour

We have now completed listing the Son of Man words in the New Testament to discover what arises out of the situations in which they occur, out of the nature of the persons to whom they are addressed, or of those who themselves speak the words. Now we shall try to deal with the contents of these statements, which should give sharper contours to the image of this being. Let us begin with two passages where the *question* about the nature of the Son of Man is raised in the text.

Following the arrival of the Greeks, John records an announcement of the Son of Man's Passion in the style peculiar to him (12:20ff). The people gather and listen. They hear that the Son of Man will die, and they ask:

> When we were taught the Law we always heard that the Christ remains and leads over into the coming aeon; so how can you say that the Son of Man must be raised up? Who is this Son of Man?'*

* Now this passage really does seem to run completely counter to the secrecy of the revelation of the Son of Man. Looked at more closely it shows: to the *disciples* Christ says, 'The hour has come for the Son of Man to be revealed in his spirit-form' (12:23); but to the crowd he says, 'When *I* have been exalted above earthly existence' (12:32), which otherwise never occurs. So he did not, after all, betray the mystery of the Son of Man to the people. It is therefore unlikely that the crowd's question took the form in which it is quoted. We must leave unresolved the problem of why the evangelist nevertheless gave it this form.

That is the direct question: Is the Messiah the same as the Son of Man? We, too, must begin with this question. Can the Christ, the Messiah, the Son of God, can the Logos die? Or is it only the man Jesus of Nazareth who dies on the cross? Could this achieve the overcoming of death and the redemption of humanity? We ask again: who is this Son of Man to whom all Passion foretellings refer? Is it only another name for Christ? Or is it the description of the being consisting of the body of Jesus of Nazareth and the spirit of the Christ which entered Jesus at the Baptism in the Jordan? Or is there yet another being beside the Son of God and the man Jesus to whom this designation 'Son of Man' refers? Christ did not give the people a direct answer. Conditions were not right for it. Even had the name Son of Man somehow been taken in by the people, it would have been merely a phrase to them. Christ declined to explain and gave only a cryptic reply. He told the people to walk in the light that would be on earth for a little while longer. After two thousand years we ask the question anew. Conditions have been different for some little time.

Mark (8:27) and Luke (9:18) bring the question which Christ puts to the disciples at Caesarea Philippi as follows:

> Who, then, do people say that I am?

This is probably how the question was phrased originally. Matthew (16:13) already has the answer contained within the way he formulates the question:

> Who, then, do people say that the Son of Man is?

It is not likely that the question was stated in this form.

Does not the whole conversation ultimately *culminate* in Christ's first revelation of himself as the Son of Man? Assuming that the text of this passage is in the original form, Matthew would have reproduced the *meaning* of the question after the event. The disciples would then have related what opinions were circulating about Christ, following his powerful speeches and deeds; it was said he that may be John the Baptist, or Elijah, or one of the prophets.

Let us imagine for a moment what really happened when Christ asked this question, first in general terms: 'Who do people say ...' and then addressed to the disciples: 'But who do you say, that I am?' It is a question for the consciousness of people in general, and then for the consciousness of the disciples and their ability to recognize an exalted spiritual being. The disciples understand that immediately. The reply which satisfies many theologians: you are Jesus of Nazareth, is not even attribute to the people by the disciples. They know that he who asks would remain anonymous even when called Jesus; and that he now wants to shed this anonymity. Peter is aware of the fact that the opinions current among the people, including, as they do, only names of former religious personalities, are not adequate. It is no reincarnated human being who walks with them here. So Peter collects himself and utters the name of the Son of God, the Messiah who is expected on earth. That is his spiritual achievement. Christ now feels that his status has been recognized, although not yet in that particular aspect which he subsequently reveals by describing himself as 'the Son of Man.' We have already noted that this revelation was followed immediately by the foretelling of Passion and death. The Son of Man is someone other than the eternal Son of God. Christ never said: I will die. Nor is he a reincarnated human being from the past, as the people believe. And yet he will die like a human being. This means that he is human because he can die, but not human in the sense that he has been active on earth before, like Elijah or John the Baptist. That much of the secret of his nature can be learned from the question concerning the Son of Man.

Lord of the Sabbath

Let us now go on to the various characterizations which Christ gives of the Son of Man. In the speech about John the Baptist (Matt.11:7–19, Luke 7:24–35) the Son of Man's nature is shown to contrast with that of John. The Baptist was an ascetic, 'did not eat bread and drank no wine.' But

> The Son of Man came and ate and drank. And now they say: See, a man who gives himself up to eating and wine-drinking, a friend of tax-collectors and outcasts.

This juxtaposition is obviously meant to show that the Son of Man is a being who does not have to fight in his soul the forces of resistance that can be overcome by asceticism. In his essential being he is untouched by earthly heaviness, darkness and temptation. Nor does he need to adhere to those regulations which, in strict Judaism and also among the Essenes, forbid association with 'unclean' people, such as tax-collectors and sinners. He cannot be classified as belonging to any of human-kind's various groups and splinter movements. He originates from beyond all classes, casts and races and is something like a common denominator of all human beings, the just and the sinners.

The Son of Man speech after the arrival of the Greeks belongs in this context, too. When Philip and Andrew report to Christ, he calls out:

> The hour has come for the Son of Man to be revealed in his spirit-form (John 12:23).

This sounds as if it was necessary that members of the nation which was then the bearer of world-culture, should approach the Son of Man first before he could see the attainment of his goal for humanity as a reality.

A similar sovereignty over everything human, even religious rules, emanates from the reply the Son of Man gives to the Pharisees as they reproach the disciples for profaning the Sabbath by plucking ears of wheat (Matt. 12:1–8, Mark 2:23–28, Luke 6:1–5). The reply: David and those who were with him ate the shewbread in the Temple when they were hungry, and priests profane the Sabbath with their Temple service.

> The Son of Man is lord even of the Sabbath.

Religious laws and commandments are for human beings who have lost their immediate relationship with the spiritual world through the Fall; whose inner moral strength is not yet sufficient for them to distinguish independently between good and evil, and who therefore need moral guidance through commandments imposed upon them. The Son of Man acts and speaks as if he has come from a condition before the Fall. He addresses that in human beings which is not yet sinful, and wants to reawaken moral autonomy in them. He allows them the same which is allowed for kings (David) and priests

(Temple service). He entered the earthly body 'without sickness' and wants to reawaken in human beings the inheritance of heaven, free from sin. We are so used to applying the concept of sinlessness to Christ, that we no longer notice what we are doing thereby. We might just as well say that God is without sin, which is almost blasphemous; for it is only meaningful and justified to stress the guiltlessness of a being, if this being were also capable of sinning. To say of the Son of God that he is without sin presupposes that it could also be otherwise. His sinlessness goes without saying. We shall see that it makes very precise sense to ascribe sinlessness to the Son of Man.

We note that in this gospel account Christ defends his *disciples* by speaking of the authority of the Son of Man. What have the disciples to do with this authority? Do they have a share in it? We shall leave this question until we come to deal with the passages where the transferability of the nature of the Son of Man, even a kind of duplication, becomes apparent.

Healer of sin

The Son of Man's relationship to the sinfulness of human beings is distinctly clarified by the words:

> The Son of Man has come (to seek and) to heal what is lost (Luke 19:10; Matt.18:11).

Or:

> The Son of Man has not come to destroy human souls but to heal them (Luke 9:55).

Sozein is the Greek word that has been translated here

as 'healing.' From this word *sotēr,* the Saviour, is derived. Here it is instructive to compare with similar statements made by Christ in the first person:

> I have not come to call upon the righteous to change their hearts and minds *(metanoia),* but rather those who are suffering from the burden of sin (Luke 5:32, compare Matt.9:13).

The difference in tone is impossible to miss. This 'I' calls imperiously. The sentence also contains a rebuke for the 'righteous,' namely the Pharisees to whom these words are addressed. It was they who had reproached the disciples and their teacher, the Christ, for sitting at table with tax-collectors and sinners. A stern judgment of their arrogance is implied by 'not the righteous.'

The Son of Man seeks and heals. Gentleness, brotherliness and also forgiveness sound in the words: 'not come to destroy human souls but to heal them.' Forgiveness, too; because this sentence is addressed to the disciples who want fire to rain down from heaven on the Samaritans who had refused Christ shelter (Luke 9:51ff). The Son of Man is closely related to the image of 'the Saviour.'

Forgiveness of sins has already been mentioned in previous passages which we included in the 'prologue' to the Son of Man proclamation (page 27):

> ... you shall see that the Son of Man has the authority to forgive sins on earth [literally: to send away, remove].

Christ speaks these words as he heals the man who is paralysed (Matt.9:1–8, Mark 2:1–12, Luke 5:17–26). This, then, is what the Son of Man claims: the power to take the consequences of sin *on earth* from people. What this means becomes clearer when we look for comparison at another meeting of Christ with a sinful person. The scribes and Pharisees brought the adulteress before him and asked if she should be stoned in accordance with the Law of Moses (John 8:3–11). Christ shames the accusers with the words: 'Whoever among you is without sin, let him cast the first stone.' Again the accusers are rejected, like the Pharisees who reproached him for eating with tax-collectors and sinners. He does not tell the adulteress that he forgives her, but that he does not condemn her. And twice he bends down and writes with his finger on the ground. That is a gesture of preserving the sin, not one of forgiveness.

At first sight this looks like a contradiction to forgiveness of sins on earth as practised by the Son of Man. But a closer look shows that, although there is a difference in attitudes, it is accounted for by the two different consequences of human transgressions. Part of these consequences relate immediately to the sinner's further life on earth. Transgressions weaken, cloud the soul, cause sickness. These consequences the Son of Man takes from us. He forgives sins *on earth*. The other part of these consequences leaves its mark on the life organism of the earth, in the cosmos. Christ indicates as much by writing on the ground. Will we be able eventually to find these marks again and erase them? So in this realm, too, there are nuances between the actions of the Son of Man and that 'I' which speaks and acts in the scene with the adulteress. The Son of Man acts as the brotherly soul of humankind, the Christ as the world's 'I.'

The Son of Man must suffer

We began this chapter by considering the question of the mortality of the Son of Man, seeing that it had been prophesied that the Messiah would remain for ever (John 12:34). Now, it is noteworthy that all foretellings of the Passion, about twenty of them, are made in the Son of Man form. With meticulous precision the distinction is made here between the Christ speaking in the first person, and the Son of Man. The following passage in John's Gospel may serve as an example:

> '... But HE who sent *me* is Truth itself, and so *I* speak out into the world what *I* have heard from HIM.' But they did not understand that he was speaking to them of the Father. And Jesus went on, 'When you lift up *the Son of Man,* then you will know that *I* am the I-AM. *I* do nothing out of myself, but *I* proclaim what the Father teaches *me.* HE who sent *me* works in *my* working. HE does not leave *me* on my own; what *I* do is always in accord with HIM.' (8:26–29).

The 'I' speaking here of God as of its Father, speaks of revealing and executing in the world what it has learned from the Father. This 'I' even uses a formula that comes close to the sublime name of God in the revelation on Mount Sinai: 'I am the I-am.' But where it speaks of Crucifixion and death — in using John's phrase: 'lifting up' — the words are about the Son of Man in the third person, and then revert immediately to the first person. This 'I' never speaks about *its* death, although there can be no doubt that it is involved in it, that indeed it also passes through this death. And yet: the one actually dying is clearly to be understood as being the Son of Man. If we note, further, that no mention is ever made of a father of the Son of Man, that the Son of Man never receives instructions from the Father God — in other words, he does not have the same relationship to the Father God as the 'I' which speaks of its Father in the heavens — then we can no longer doubt that here we have a precise differentiation.

Another example of this strict differentiation is the account of the disciples' quarrel about rank. According to Matthew (20:28), Christ's replied:

> The Son of Man has not come to be served but to serve and to offer up his soul for the salvation of many.

Mark uses similar words (10:45). Luke, however, who reports the speech in the first person, also omits the prophecy of death:

> I am in your midst as one who serves (22:27).

Instead of the foretelling of the Passion there follows the promise:

> You shall eat and drink at my table in this kingdom that I bring: you shall sit on the twelve thrones as guides of the destiny of the twelve tribes of the people of God (22:30).

In the light of all this we have to advance to a view of human nature for which we usually have no need — with one exception which we shall deal with presently; namely the perception of a being whose 'I' relates differently to other parts of its being than the human 'I' relates to the members of *its* being. It is true that we humans can say: 'my soul' and thereby differentiate between the speaking 'I' and its soul. But with this formulation we express 'ownership' rather than giving the soul the character of a separate person. It is different with children under the age of three. They talk about themselves in the third person: 'Johnny wants that.' And the reason for this is that the 'I' has not yet entered all parts of the child's being, that there actually still are two separate entities: the child incarnated as far as the soul, and the not yet incarnated 'I.' As regards the 'I' and its relationship to the Son of Man, we evidently have to assume a condition that lies somewhere between those two human possibilities: neither a possessive relationship like ours to the soul, nor differentiation in the sense of 'outside' or 'side by side' as with small children. And yet a distinction which comes to expression in the fact that the Christ 'I' is like a son to the Father God and, in the speeches delivered in the first person, does not identify with the suffering, dying Son of Man.

The Son of God must have a reason for speaking of the Son of Man in the third person.

In the series of predictions of the Son of Man's Passion, death and Resurrection, there is a growing intensity which, by and large, accords with the sequence of the accounts in the gospels. The first predictions are veiled. Already before Peter's confession Matthew speaks of the 'sign of Jonah':

> But no other wonder will be given to it, except the sign of the prophet Jonah. As Jonah was three days and three nights within the fish, so the Son of Man will lie for three days and three nights in the heart of the earth. (12:39f).

Luke has this speech in a shorter version (11:29f). The audience — in Matthew it is the scribes and Pharisees, in Luke the people or 'the crowd' — would not have interpreted this comparison with the prophet Jonah as indicating the death of the Son of Man. The scribes may perhaps still have known that the images of Jonah's experience stood for supersensory occurrences; the people knew at any rate that Jonah did not died then. Christ concealed the future destiny of the Son of Man more than he revealed it. However, the prophecy that the Son of Man would be three days and three nights in the heart of the earth showed that this was something more and greater than what happened to the prophet who was 'in the belly of the whale.' Jonah's experience concerned only himself, the destiny of the Son of Man concerned the whole earth.

The other veiled allusion to the Passion is in the conversation with Nicodemus:

> And as Moses lifted up the serpent in the wilderness, so must the Son of Man be lifted up, so that all who feel his power in their hearts may win a share of the life that is beyond time (John 3:14f).

The serpent was the symbol for an old magic type of consciousness which proved to be decadent and harmful during the people of Israel's wanderings in the desert.* When Moses lifted up the bronze serpent as a sign what took place was a healing and a raising of the forces of the soul and of consciousness. The initiate Nicodemus, hearing that the Son of Man was to be lifted up like that bronze serpent, is more likely to have thought of the

* See Emil Bock, *The Three Years,* p.168f.

beginning of a new path of knowledge rather than bodily death and Resurrection.

Of all the foretellings of the Passion these two allusions — in the sign of Jonah and of the serpent — show most directly that the death and Resurrection of the Son of Man will have an effect on the state of humanity's consciousness. They relate to the 'esoteric' consequences of the mystery of Golgotha. In view of this the remaining foretellings of the Passion, which concentrate more on predicting the outer circumstances, appear less obvious.

Matthew (17) and Mark (9) record a Passion prophecy which was made one week after the event of Caesarea Philippi, that is, just after the Transfiguration. There Christ draws a parallel between the lot of the Son of Man and the destiny of Elijah-John. Although Christ here speaks first of the Son of Man's rising from the dead, this did not necessarily have to be understood in the sense of a violent death. The disciples raise the objection that surely Elijah first had to come. Christ replied:

> 'Elijah has already come, and human beings did not recognize him but treated him according to their whim ...' Then the disciples understood that he was speaking to them of John the Baptist (Matt.17:12f).

And thereby they could also understand that the Son of Man would be killed like John the Baptist.

Luke is more specific about the outer circumstances already at Peter's confession. The Son of Man will be:

> scorned and killed by the elders and chief priests and scribes (9:22).

Mark mentions the same persecutors (8:31). Matthew

speaks of chief priests and scribes (20:18) and so does Mark (10:33). More general statements are: 'the Son of Man will be delivered into the hands of men.' (Matt. 17:22; Mark 9:31; Luke 9:44); 'into the hands of the enemies of God' (Mark 14:41); 'handed over to the foreign peoples' (Matt.20:19; Luke 18:32). Seen historically it is self-evident that human beings must shoulder the guilt of having caused the Crucifixion. So self-evident that there is no reason for the gospels to mention it in the foretellings of the Passion. Where it happens nevertheless, we may assume that something is being said, over and above the external facts. And that, too, happens only in Christ's Son of Man speeches. It is the Son of Man who falls into the hands of human beings, it is he, also, who suffers and dies. It is as if Christ's relationship to human beings on earth is mediated by the Son of Man, in both a positive and a negative sense. The Son of Man eats with the tax-collectors and sinners (see pages 35f). But he is also accessible to his enemies. And they, in turn, seem like representatives of all humankind, of 'sinners,' of 'humans,' of 'heathens' (literally: of peoples). If anything can clear up the debate about the guilt of the Jews who brought about the Crucifixion, it is the fact that, in the Passion prophecies taken as a whole, the chief priests and scribes are shown as representatives of all humankind, expressly including other nations; the guilt is not that of the Jews alone. As Son of Man, Christ is no *deus ex machina*. Humanity is player and antagonist in his drama. He has an affinity to the human being as such, and involves not only poor sinners but also opponents in his working.

Luke records his last words in Son of Man form. They no longer belong to the foretellings of the Passion but are found in the scene with which the Passion begins, when what had been foretold takes place. As Judas, in the garden of Gethsemane, gives the sign that identifies Christ, Christ asks him:

> Judas, do you betray the Son of Man with a kiss? (Luke 22:48).

Leaving aside, for the moment, the dreadfulness of the deed, and taking it beyond the moral plane as symbol in the destiny of humanity, we find something else expressed by it. The Son of Man is brought near to the fulfilment of his deed of redemption by a human being through the most intimate sign of human closeness. Christ touches upon the moral aspect of this deed in the words spoken earlier:

> Woe to him by whom the Son of Man is betrayed (Matt.26:24; Mark 14:21; Luke 22:22).

This woe begins with Judas' suicide. At the same time, this traitor's kiss, regarded as a sign, a rune of the history of humanity, also means this: touched by a human being's gesture of love, the Son of Man takes the first step on the path of his Passion.*

* If we can imagine that Judas expected quite different results to flow from his actions, that he wanted to compel the Messiah, now in the hands of the powers of this world, at long last to reveal his own might and restore the old Jewish kingdom, then the Judas kiss no longer seems merely a sign of treachery or a misuse of such a gesture. He may still have clung to his master in intimate reverence and love and have wished to do him a service, albeit by force. The fateful error in his understanding of the Messiah made him see his action as grim declaration of faith, not as a betrayal. Looked at like this, the question, 'With a kiss do you betray the *Son of Man?*' may have been the moment when Judas should have realized his mistake; for it had not been prophesied of the Son of Man that he would fulfil those Messiah expectations which Judas held in his heart, but rather that he would be killed and offer no resistance to this destiny. If this is so, then Christ's question contains the same teaching for Judas as was given to Peter at Caesarea Philippi.

The speeches in John's Gospel which correspond to the Passion prophecies in the synoptic gospels, have a different tone. And not only that, they are also different in content, although they, too, allude to the Passion. Beginning with the first prediction of death made to Nicodemus (3:14), these speeches say that the Son of Man will be *lifted up*, (8:28) or that he will be *revealed* in his spirit-form (12:23; 13:31). The focus is not on the earthly aspect of the Passion, not the suffering, being killed, being crucified. And consequently the persons who bring about the Passion are not mentioned, either. The Johannine expressions 'lifting up' and 'revealing' refer to the inner, the spiritual aspect of the Mystery of Golgotha. A glimmer of that which follows, the radiance of the Resurrection and Ascension already illumines the sacrifice of the Son of Man. Strangely, the numerous predictions found in the synoptic gospels concerning the future heavenly Son of Man, are missing altogether in John's Gospel. John reduces the motif of lifting up and revealing to a metamorphosis of the Passion prophecies, thereby, in a certain sense, anticipating it.

He will rise again

In the Son of Man speeches of the synoptic gospel writers there are four images which go beyond the Crucifixion into the future: Resurrection, sitting on the celestial throne, judgment motifs and the Second Coming. These images of the future, too, refer, almost without exception, to the Son of Man. The exceptions, when Christ speaks once in the first person of his Resurrection (Matt.26:32) and twice of his Second Coming (John 14:3 and 18:21f), provide an opportunity to notice once more that the Christ

'I' cannot be separated from the Son of Man, either as regards the person or regarding the mission. Christ speaks of the Son of Man as of something within himself, intimately belonging to him, a part of himself. So therefore he can also, on occasion, say something in the first person which at other times he says about the Son of Man. The fact that this happens especially with images that relate to spiritual conditions and events after the death on Golgotha, may perhaps also be a sign that the Son of Man experiences a development through death and Resurrection. But on the other hand it is impossible to overlook that, almost without exception, Christ himself mentions the Son of Man when speaking of suffering, death, Resurrection, sitting at the right hand of God, the Second Coming and the Last Judgment.

After having established all these characteristics of the Son of Man, we may be surprised to find that he is also supposed to be the Risen One. We think of the Christ 'I' as the Risen One, and in that we are right. He says so himself in the first person on one occasion. However, in his Son of Man speeches he evidently deems it important to convey that the entity named 'Son of Man' also goes through death and resurrection, as if this ultimately were crucial. The following consideration may help us a step further: at the Baptism in the Jordan, the human 'I' that had lived in the earthly body of Jesus of Nazareth, left it. The Christ spirit entered in its place. Therefore, it could not be a human 'I' which rose from the dead after the Crucifixion, but about the Son God there was never any doubt. We cannot even imagine that a divine being would not survive death. Could it be that an intermediate member was needed between the divine being and the human body, in order to give both the death on the cross and the Resurrection the character and the special power of redeeming earthly humanity? An intermediary as a kind of 'trans-former'?

In the images of the Son of Man enthroned in heaven, it is striking that here, too, he is not brought into direct relationship with the Father God (see pages 41f). He will sit on the throne of his glory *(doxa)* (Matt.19:28; 25:31). Or he will sit at the right hand of power *(dynamis)* (Matt. 26:64; Mark 14:62). Luke expands: At the right hand of the divine power (22:69). This is not the place to investigate the meaning of *doxa* or *dynamis*. *Doxa* appears in the throne images as honour or a quality that is inherent in the Son of Man himself. It is '*his* doxa.' 'Dynamis,' on the other hand, is a power or power-being belonging to God. The formula 'on the right hand of God,' familiar from the Creed, does not occur in that form in the gospels. Christ did not use it. In these speeches the Son of Man does not appear in such close proximity to the Father God. The formulation in Luke: 'at the right hand of the divine dynamis' also avoids the full immediacy of the Creed formula. This formula only occurs in the Letters. There it refers to Christ, not to the Son of Man. In this respect, too, a differentiation is made between Christ and the Son of Man. Yet here again there is *one* exception. Stephen sees 'the Son of Man at the right hand of God' (Acts 7:56).

This exception confirms once more that there is no reason to assume that the Christ 'I' is separate from the Son of Man.

He will come anew

The prophecies of the *coming* of the Son of Man initially have the simple form: 'he is coming' (Matt.10:23) and then expand in two directions: with whom he comes and under what circumstances.

He comes with great power and glory (Matt.24:30; Mark 13:26; Luke 21:27). Mark and Luke (not Matthew) qualify the *dynamis* as 'great.' This changes the meaning of *dynamis.* In the image of sitting at the right hand of the *dynamis,* or the *dynamis* of God (see above), it appeared as an entity external to the Son of Man. Through the adjective 'great' it is presented as an authority transferred to him.

Conversely, a change in the significance of *doxa* occurs in the prophecy:

> he will come in the *doxa* of *his* Father (Mark 8:38, compare Matt.16:27).

Luke has a different version:

> he will reveal himself in his 'doxa' *and* in the 'doxa' *of* the Father (9:26).

Luke also has the *doxa* appear as a quality of the Son of Man at the Second Coming; furthermore, it is distinguished from the *doxa* of the Father by the word 'and,' whereas in Matthew and Mark it is regarded as something emanating from the Father and enveloping the Son of Man. The *doxa,* the light of revelation that belongs to the Son of Man alone in the throne images, now has its origin in the Father or (with Luke) belongs to both the Father and the Son of Man. The Son of Man moves closer to the Father God the further the prophecies reach into the future. The descriptions of the Coming also involve a second circumstance: now the Son of Man becomes the Son of the Father (Matt.16:27; Mark 8:38).

The Coming One is attended by angels. This prophecy, too, appears in different forms. In one case the angels are described only as such:

> he will come ... surrounded by all angels (Matt.25:31).
>
> ... with all the realms of the angels (Luke 9:26; compare Mark 8:38).

But then the angels are also brought into a direct relationship with the Son of Man:

> he will come with *his* angels [the angels who serve him] (Matt.16:27).

as already previously:

> he will send out the angels who serve him (Matt.13:41, compare 24:31).

This makes the Son of Man into a spiritual being who is attended by angels whom he can command; who therefore must have a higher rank. Already in the teaching given to Nathanael the angels are mentioned as companions of the Son of Man:

> You will see heaven opened, and the angels of God ascending and descending above the Son of Man. (John 1:51).

In this way it is made known to the initiate from Galilee that a new day has dawned for beholding the spiritual world. The opened heaven consists of beings, of angels. 'Heavenly forces ascending and descending and handing each other golden buckets' (Goethe) can again be beheld because of the presence of the Son of Man. For Nathanael, this 'ascending and descending above the Son of Man' could not mean that he would see angels approach the human figure of Jesus of Nazareth and ascend from it again. For reasons which we shall get to know, he understood: the Son of Man must be present in the soul of the beholder for such visions to be possible.

The manner of the Son of Man's Coming is foretold in dramatic pictures and similes.

> For the spiritual coming *(perousia)* of the Son of Man will be like the lightning which flashes up in the East and shines out as far as the West (Matt.24:27).
>
> For the Son of Man in his day will be like the lightning which flashes up in one part of the sky and yet instantly pours out its bright light over the whole firmament (Luke 17:24).
>
> He comes at an unexpected hour (Matt.24:44, compare Luke 12:40).
>
> The time in which the Son of Man reveals himself will be like the days of (Matt.24:37, compare Luke 17:26).
>
> As when fire and sulphur rained down upon Sodom, so will it be on the day when the Son of Man is revealed ... (Luke 17:30).

Generally, we expect the Second Coming of *Christ,* and indeed he promised it, using the first person (John 14:3, 18, 28). That this promise, before the farewell discourses in the circle of the disciples, is always delivered in the *Son of Man* form receives no particular attention. In the course of this study we shall try to become aware, from the overall picture of the Son of Man which emerges from Christ's words, whether there are perhaps nuances particular to all the events described or foretold by the Christ 'I' or by the Son of Man, according to which form is used to describe them. In the case of the Second Coming *(parousia)* it should be noted that the dramatic warnings — like lightning, sulphur over Sodom, the Flood — are issued in the Son of Man form.

In two speeches about the Son of Man we find the motif of coming in the *clouds* (Matt.24:30; Mark 13:26; Luke 21:27 and Matt.26:64; Mark 14:62). We shall return to this when we have become acquainted with the origin of the Son of Man concept. In the Revelation to John we see the Son of Man sitting on a cloud (14:14), an image of the future fulfilment of this promise.

A further group of promises claims authority of decision over human souls for the Son of Man. One of these passages may serve as a key to the others.

> *And because he is also the Son of Man,* [the Father] has given him authority to make the decisions about destinies (John 5:27).

That makes it clear: it is of the greatest significance that the Christ 'I' includes the Son of Man as a quality, an intrinsic part or as a power. At the end of time it is Christ, not as such, but as the bearer or possessor of 'the Son of Man' who decides the destiny of souls.

There is a special kind of intimacy in the descriptions of this event. In a preview of the Son of Man sitting on a throne is already stated:

> In the sphere of new birth where the Son of Man sits on the throne of his *doxa,* you who

> have followed me will also sit on twelve thrones and be the guides of destiny for the twelve tribes of Israel (Matt.19:28).

The Son of Man shares his authority with the disciples who have followed him:

> And he will send out his angels ... and they will gather together all those who are united with him as bearers of the higher being (Matt. 24:31).

There is a special intimacy in a series of passages in Luke:

> Blessed are you, you who are hated, shunned and reviled by men, ... for the sake of the Son of Man (6:22).
>
> Whoever does not unite himself with my Being and with the words that I speak, with him the Son of Man will not unite, either (9:26, compare Mark 8:38).

In this sentence the speech in the first person changes to the Son of Man form in a characteristic manner: the Word (logos) and 'the words' are of Christ, not of the Son of Man. And the latter judges by human standards: he spurns those who spurn him.

> When someone acknowledges before other human beings that he lives in my Being, the Son of Man will also make it known that he lives in him, and this he will acknowledge in the sight of all angels of God (Luke 12:8).

The object of the acknowledgement, of the confession,

is Christ, the Son of God. The brotherly confessor in the spiritual worlds is the Son of Man. But he is also the yardstick against which the merit of souls is measured:

> So be of wakeful spirit at all times, school your souls in prayer, so that you may become strong to live through all that is coming without being harmed, and to be able to stand before the revelation of the Son of Man (Luke 21:36).

The Son of Man as mediator for Christ

Let us now summarize what has emerged as an outline of the images of the Son of Man. By his attitude towards the commandment of honouring the Sabbath, the laws concerning food and the commandment not to associate with sinners, the Son of Man testifies that, by virtue of his origin and his nature, he is of the time before the Fall and thereby before the Law came into effect. As a being whose relationship to all human beings is like that of Goethe's archetypal plant to all species of plant; as 'archetypal human being' he associates with initiates and sinners, with Jews and Greeks. His fate must be prepared through the 'hands of human beings.' He is a healer of humanity which suffers from the sickness of sin. But he does not heal* or raise people from the dead; that is done by the Christ 'I' by virtue of his Logos power. The mission of the Son of Man is the healing of souls in the long term with the end of the earth in mind, when he will

* The healing of the paralytic (Matt.9:1–8; Mark 2:1–12; Luke 5:17–26) appears to be an exception to this. True, in that incident is to be demonstrated that 'the Son of Man has authority to forgive sins' — but the one who proves this forgiveness of sin visibly, right into the physical body, is Christ himself, as it is in all other healings.

gather in the harvest of the earth with his sickle (Rev. 14:14). It is no contradiction that he 'forgives sins on earth.' Forgiveness is not yet a healing of the soul.

The Son of Man is never called Son of God. The Son of God is the Christ 'I.' It is Christ who has the listening and obedient relationship to the Father God, not the Son of Man. All prophecies to do with suffering, death, sitting at the right hand of God and judgment, relate to the Son of Man, as do most foretellings of the Resurrection and the Second Coming. Of course the Christ 'I' also participates in all this, and yet it seems that the Son of Man is needed as mediator in order that humanity may reap the benefit of the deed of redemption. It seems equally important that the Son of Man is to rise from the dead and take on a mission in the spiritual world. This mission is so far-reaching that the Father God transfers the authority to pronounce judgment to Christ, because he is the Son of Man (John 5:27).

The differentiation between the ego-bearing Son of God and the Son of Man is no more strict and exclusive in Christ's speeches than it is in Christ's own nature. Yet it is consistently distinct and characteristic. The speech recorded in Matthew as well as Luke may serve as a last illustration of this. In slightly varied form the following sentence appears:

> The word which someone speaks against the Son of Man can be forgiven him; but if he directs it against the Holy Spirit, it cannot be forgiven him (Matt.12:32).

From the context in Luke it becomes particularly clear that Christ identifies himself with the Son of Man; for here the preceding sentence reads:

> When someone acknowledges before other human beings that he lives in my Being, the Son of Man will also make it known that he lives in him, and this he will acknowledge in the sight of all angels of God (Luke 12:8).

From the changed mode of speech (my Being — Son of Man) we can learn even more than from the passage mentioned above (page 53). Although the gospels speak about faith in the Son of Man, they never mention bearing witness, confessing to him. These are, of course, two different attitudes of soul. To Christ is due the active 'confessing before men.' Concerning the nature of relations to the Son of Man, however, Christ twice puts this as a question:

> Do you trust [believe] in the Son of Man? (John 9:35).
>
> When the Son of Man comes will he find the necessary inner strength [faith] in human beings living on the earth? (Luke 18:8).

Once again, the differentiation is clear. The Son of Man is not the 'master,' the *kyrios,* who appoints disciples. He is the quiet guest who waits to be invited. But it is also he who, as it were, presents the angels with humanity's confession to Christ, that is to say, makes it radiate forth from their souls. *He* declares himself *for humanity*, he himself shines forth from their hearts.

Now what does the subsequent sentence say about forgiveness for one who speaks against the Son of Man? Clearly, this designates the Son of Man as a being who does not claim divine rank over human beings, as does the Holy Spirit. One cannot imagine the sentence to read 'whoever denies *me* ...' At any rate, it is not what it says. And so it seems, once more, that the Son of Man occupies a middle position between God and human beings. It is no blasphemy to speak against him; but since he must be imagined intimately bound up with Christ, he appears as a connecting link which extends simultaneously into human being and Christ.

The Son of Man and the disciples

We must now look at a number of passages in which the image of the Son of Man is enlarged in a surprising way. The episode of the disciples picking ears of wheat on the Sabbath has left a question open (page 36). Not Christ but his disciples have broken the Sabbath commandment. And Christ defends them with the words:

> The Son of Man is lord even of the Sabbath (Matt.12:8).

Modern theology has come to the conclusion that the expression 'Son of Man' takes on a collective meaning here; that is, the disciples are included. This is clearly true, yet it does not provide a real explanation. Instead we must assume that 'Son of Man' is a characteristic which can be transferred to the disciples and that this power is not restricted to an entity which is part of the nature of Christ; rather, it can be duplicated, as it were. Only when the disciples shall have attained the rank of Son of Man themselves will these words defend them in reality.

The reply given by Christ to Nicodemus points in the same direction. The subject of the conversation is the path that leads to 'beholding the kingdom of God,' to perceiving the spiritual world. Christ speaks of being born anew in the Spirit. Nicodemus does not yet understand. Then follow the words:

> No one has ascended into the world of spirit who has not also descended out of the world of spirit; that is the Son of Man (John 3:13).

If Christ here were referring only to himself, it would mean that the gates of the spiritual world are closed to all human beings. However, that cannot be his meaning, since he previously spoke of a spiritual rebirth as a possible way of entering the world of the spirit. We can only take the sentence to mean that an initiate must become 'Son of Man' in order to reach his goal. In this way, Son of Man becomes an entity or power which is joined to Christ in a special sense, but which can also arise in human souls.

Confirmation of this can be seen in an image of the future outlined by Christ. He says to the disciples:

> In the sphere of new birth where the Son of Man sits on the throne of his light-revelation, you who have followed me will also sit on twelve thrones and be the guides of destiny for the twelve tribes of Israel (Matt.19:28).

In this image we see the authority of the Son of Man transferred to the disciples, not only to honour them but as strength for their mission to humanity.

In the speech recorded by Matthew (25:31–46) the secret is revealed of how the Son of Man is connected to individual human souls. It is the foretelling of the judgment over which the Son of Man will one day preside. Christ lets this Son of Man justify his decisions by having him say:

> I was hungry and you gave me to eat; I was
> thirsty and you gave me to drink (Matt.25:35)

and so on. And in explanation the Son of Man then says:

> What you did for the least of my brothers, that
> did for me (25:40).

Thereby the Son of Man characterizes himself as a being whose nature it is to extend his perception into each individual human soul, irrespective of whether the individual souls want to form a relationship with him or not. Here the Son of Man appears as the soul of humanity. He is present as an unnoticed guest in individual souls, but he can awaken in them and make each human being a Son of Man.

Christ speaks of Sons of Man in the plural in a last speech from which we quote here:

> Yes, I say to you: All transgressions can be
> forgiven the sons of men, even the misuse of
> the Word (Mark 3:28).

Once the rank of Son of Man has been attained, then a power which is stronger than the sickness of sin has found room in the soul because it is itself beyond the reach of the effects of the Fall.

Let us mention already now the second passage in the New Testament where there is mention of a plurality of Sons of Man:

> the Christ mystery, which was not made known
> to mankind [the sons of men] in bygone ages,
> but which now has been revealed in the spirit
> to his holy apostles and prophets (Eph.3:4f).

Paul knew that in past generations there were human beings who, although they had established a relationship with the Son of Man which entitled them to be called by that name themselves, could not yet be aware of Christ. Here, too, we find that there is a differentiation in time between the revelation of the Son of Man and that of Christ. A further reason why we have to distinguish between the two, despite them later being within one another. We have still to get to know the Sons of Man of previous generations.

3. The Son of Man in the Old Testament

So far we have tried to gain an insight from the New Testament, and in particular from the sayings of Christ, into the deeper levels of the designation 'Son of Man.' Let us now investigate the meaning of the word as such, and then its pre-history in the Old Testament and its Apocrypha.

A main obstacle to understanding the term Son of Man has been that it was regarded in an abstract-grammatical way, rather than as a word-image, a not uncommon usage of language in the past. Other, similar phrases from oriental languages were drawn on for comparison, such as: 'Son of Lies,' 'Son of Riches,' etc.; and the conclusion was reached that they meant no more than: a liar, a rich man. But even abstractly understood this is not correct. A rich man is not necessarily a 'Son of Riches.' That designation means that a man is dominated and moulded by his riches, that his character is a product of his wealth. Similar expressions are also to be found in the New Testament. In Luke 10:6 there is a reference to a 'Son of Peace' upon whom the peace of the apostles can rest. This does not simply mean a man who receives the apostles in a friendly manner, but one who has learned to master the emotional stirrings of his soul. Although peace, *eirēnē,* is no longer personified in the New Testament as it was in classical antiquity, it is nevertheless not regarded merely as a state of soul, but as a soul substance which can even be transferred to others. This is expressed in a formula such as 'peace be to this house' (Luke 10:6). A 'Son of Peace' is a personality who is a product of peace. In this sense, the 'son of the human being' [the 'Son of Man'] is not just another human being, but a being who has yet to emerge from the present-day human being as an outcome of the evolution of mankind.

The term Son of Man appears first in its Aramaic form *bar-nasha,* or in the Hebrew form *ben-adam,* in those books of the Old Testament which have come down to us under the names of two prophets. These prophets lived with the people of Israel in the Babylonian captivity in the sixth century BC. They are Daniel and Ezekiel.

Daniel

In the seventh chapter of the Book of Daniel a tremendous apocalyptic vision is described. It leads the seer into the turbulent etheric realm: over the 'great sea' the four winds rage against one another. Then, one by one, four animals emerge from the sea, a lion, a bear, a panther and an unnamed animal 'terrible, dreadful and exceedingly strong.' In the subsequent interpretation they are explained as 'four kingdoms' which perish one after the other.* Then comes a solemn scene: chairs are brought and the divine being seats himself on a throne of fire and dispenses judgment. It is noteworthy that this exalted being is called neither Yahweh, nor any other Jewish name, but is named as 'the Ancient of Days,' an Iranian-Persian expression. Then the vision continues:

* See Bock, *Kings and Prophets.*

> And, behold, with the cloud of heaven there came one *like a Son of Man,* and he came to the Ancient of Days and was presented before him. And to him was given dominion and glory and kingdom, that all people, nations and languages should serve him; his authority is an everlasting dominion which shall not pass away, and his kingdom on that shall not be destroyed. (7:13f).

'He came with the clouds of heaven' is a literal reminder of the prophecies in the gospels, for example:

> they shall see the Son of Man coming on the clouds of heaven (Matt.24:30 RSV).

Christ Jesus often shows that he is familiar with the books of the Old Testament. Is it possible that he quoted Daniel merely to apply a beautiful picture for the coming of the Son of Man? Or is he saying that the Son of Man of whom he speaks, is the one Daniel saw? Be that as it may, the images that the Son of Man was perceived in the etheric world six hundred years before Christ's incarnation, as he will be at his Second Coming in the future.

No satisfactory explanation has yet been found for the Greek formulation *hōs huios anthropou,* like the son of a human being, (it conforms exactly to the original Aramaic text.) A similar formula in the Revelation to John raises the same question: *homoion huion anthropou,* [I saw] one who was similar to, or like, a Son of Man (1:13; 14:14). The answer seems to be that the comparative words *hōs* and *homoion* ('like' and 'similar to') refer only to *huios* (Son) and not to *huios anthropou* (Son of Man) as a whole. The meaning would then be: an entity that relates to the human being like a son: a being that has yet to emerge from *the* human being (humanity). And with that our interpretation of the term Son of Man (see above) would be confirmed.

In the vision of Daniel the Son of Man is contrasted with the animals who dominate their 'kingdoms' as increasingly wicked powers and then perish. The 'day and the hour' of the duration of their dominion has been predetermined for the animals. The kingdom of the Son of Man, however, encompasses all of humanity, and his authority extends across aeons. It would be quite natural for us to equate the Son of Man with Christ *per se* (see above, page 36). If, in the course of our investigation this equation should prove not to be valid without certain reservations, then we shall have discovered another characteristic of the Son of Man as a separate being. It is surely striking that the Son of Man, who as yet is without the connection to Christ, is placed by Daniel above all nations, races and kingdoms, and this at a time when the only gods venerated were those who guided individual nations. All-encompassing humanness is the essence of this being.

We have noticed that in some passages of the New Testament, the concept 'Son of Man' shows the tendency to widen its scope beyond the single entity to include a number of human beings, and even to appear as a plural, 'the Sons of Man' (page 58). For the being himself this means that, despite his obvious characteristics as a person, he can nevertheless extend into a greater number of human beings and, by raising them to his own rank, include them in his own compass, as it were.

In the Book of Daniel we find a counterpart to this. After the appearance of the Son of Man in the clouds, the prophet turns to one of the 'ten thousand times ten thousand' who stand before the Ancient of Days, and asks for an interpretation of his vision. In this interpretation the four animals appear as the images of the group souls of four 'kingdoms,' that is, historical groups of human beings. In the vision, the power which replaces the four animals is the Son of Man, but in the interpretation it is 'the holy people of the Most High' (7:25), who are thereby equated with the Son of Man.

Between, on the one hand, the groups of people or nations which constitute the kingdoms of the animals in this vision, and the 'saints of the Most High' (7:18) on the other, there is a characteristic difference of relationship to the rulers of the kingdoms. The human beings associated with the kingdoms of the animals are not mentioned, just as if they were indistinguishable from the group souls of the animals; whereas in the subsequent kingdom of the Son of Man, the 'saints of the Most High' have reached such a degree of maturity that together they are named in place of the Son of Man. The Son of Man duplicates himself through the individualization of human souls.

The judgment motif also figures already in the Book of Daniel in connection with the coming of the Son of Man. After his appearing,

> the Ancient of Days came and gave authority to judge to the saints of the Most High. The crucial time *(kairos)* arrived and the saints received the kingdom. (7:22).

Not the Son of Man himself, but the saints of the Most High are appointed as judges, as will be the case with the apostles at a later time (Matt.19:28; see above, page 59).

Ezekiel

The visionary experience of Ezekiel is of a different kind, although it is apparent that it concerns the same supersensory subject. Here we meet the four animals who are familiar to us as symbols of the evangelists. Daniel saw the four evil animals in chronological sequence. Ezekiel beholds eagle, lion, bull and human being simultaneously. They are placed in space. They go 'straight forward,' they 'darted to and fro,' 'they went in any of their four directions,' they 'rose,' they 'stood.' They are characterized by interacting in space. The seer hears their movements: the rustle of their wings is like the sound of a many waters and between the sounds 'the voice of the Word *[phonē tou logou]* like the voice of a war lord.'

Here it is necessary to anticipate the last chapter of this book, in which our subject will be scrutinized in the light of Anthroposophy. Ezekiel's four animals known to the Jews from the symbolism of the Temple of Jerusalem and later appearing as the four symbols of the evangelists are images of four cosmic forces which worked together in the creation of the human organism: the forces of the 'eagle' engendered the sense-nerve system, the forces of the 'lion' the central rhythmic system (heart and lungs), the forces of the 'bull' metabolism and limbs, and the 'human' or angel forces brought harmony and unity to the whole. The three bodily systems provide the physical bases for thinking (eagle), feeling (lion) and the will (bull), which are unified through a fourth force (human being). So, what Ezekiel sees are the forces which give form to the human being. They represent the fourfold differentiation of that superior power which the Prologue to John's Gospel calls the Creator of all that has been created, the Logos, the cosmic Word. It is, therefore, quite correct when the Codex Vaticanus (Codex B) has the voice of the Logos accompany the activity of the four animals as if co-ordinating *(parembolē)* — even though this passage may have been inserted later in Christian times.*

In heaven, above the four animals, Ezekiel beholds the image of a throne as of sapphire upon which sits a being like the

> archetype of a human being from above *[hōs eidos anthropou anōthen]* (1:26).

Ezekiel does not use the term Son of Man. Christian theology has accustomed us to apply the relevant passages from the books of the prophets directly to the Christ as a unified being. However, if we take this vision as it is, it would better fit the Zarathustran archetypal human, whose relationship to the Son of Man has already been discovered by theological research. We shall deal further with this question when looking at Ezra and Enoch.

A peculiarity of the Book of Ezekiel is that the term 'Son of Man' returns repeatedly in a different sense. Ezekiel himself is addressed as such by the One sitting enthroned, as often as the inspirer turns to him. It is *the prophet* upon whom this rank is bestowed. We have already seen that 'Son of Man' not only describes a single being, but, as an attainment, can be transferred to others (page 58). In this sense Ezekiel is given a place among the Sons of Man before this concept appeared in Christianity. He is of the rank of the 'saints of God' mentioned in the Book of Daniel.†

* Codex Vaticanus dates from the fourth Christian century.

† Origen calls Ezekiel the 'Son of Man' *per se* (*Ezekiel Homilies* XIV.1).

We have already mentioned the relevant passage in Paul's letter (page 60) from which it is evident that he, living in the first Christian century, knew that in the past there had been people who, although they could not yet behold the Christ, were nevertheless familiar with the Son of Man and were named after him (Eph.3:5). In Ezekiel we have such a seer before us; he is awarded the title Son of Man. Looking for confirmation in Anthroposophy for that which Paul still knew, we find it in the following passage by Rudolf Steiner:

> This soul [the Son of Man] is not one that could be encountered as a physical human being; it could only be perceived by the seers of old. They could behold it; it frequented the mysteries, as it were.*

Ezra

Ezra was among the seers of old. The setting for Ezekiel's vision was the sphere of cosmic fire. Like Daniel's vision, that of the Fourth Book of Ezra† takes us towards the storm-lashed ether-sea.

> In my dream, a wind arose from the sea and set all its waves in turmoil. As I watched, the wind brought a figure like that of a man out of the depths, and he flew with the clouds of heaven. (2 Esdras 13:2f REB).

* *The Bhagavad Gita and the Epistles of Paul,* lecture 5.

† The canonical Book of Ezra is continued in the apocryphal Esdras, the Fourth Book of Ezra being equivalent to 2 Esdras.

The fourfold ordering of space, which we noted in Ezekiel, appears in Ezra in a negative sense.

> Next I saw a countless host of men gathering from the four winds of heaven to vanquish the man who had come up out of the sea. ... He had no spear in his hand, no weapon at all; only, as I watched, he poured out what appeared to be a stream of fire from his mouth, a breath of flame from his lips ... which fell upon the host prepared for battle, and burnt them all up. (2 Esdras 13:5, 9–11).

That this nevertheless is not an act of violence on the part of the Son of Man becomes clear from the following interpretation of the image:

> The day is near when the Most High will start bringing deliverance to those on earth. Its panic-stricken inhabitants will plot hostilities against one another, city against city, region against region, nation against nation, kingdom against kingdom. (2 Esdras 13:29–31).

What is meant here is that, as a dark background to the appearance of the Son of Man, the mutual self-destruction of humanity takes place.

The heavenly fire surrounding the Ancient of Days sitting on his throne, as seen by Daniel (7:9), appears to Ezekiel like a circular glow of fire, surrounding the Son of Man as an aura (1:27). Ezra has the fire inhabit this being, as it were, bursting forth as a force that has the effect of a fire of wrath upon his enemies. In Christ it becomes the flame of love which he brings to the earth.

> I have come to cast a fire at the earth; I have no other wish than to see it burning already (Luke 12:49).

From Ezra we can gain another insight into the destiny of the Son of Man. In the interpretation of the vision is said:

> The man you saw coming up from the heart of the sea is he whom the Most High has held in readiness during many ages; through him he will deliver the world he has made (2 Esdras 13:25f).

In this way the Son of Man is shown as a being who has been retained in the spiritual world since the days of creation; a being who did not become involved in the Fall and who therefore can act as a healing power. From the Christian point of view now one immediately again thinks of Christ himself, who, after all, only entered Creation as a human being at the midpoint of the aeons. Ezra himself seems to promote this idea. The Son of Man is repeatedly called 'my Son' by the Most High. (2 Esdras 13:32, 37, 52). The image of the Son of Man as it appears to Ezra unites with the concept of a Son of God. But let us consider that Ezra did not find the idea or expectation of a Son of God in Judaism, that even the Messiah was not thought of as such. On the other hand, it would have been quite impossible for Jewish religious feelings to associate the idea of a Son of God with a being who is as close to being human as the one described as 'Son of Man' or simply 'man.' The inspirations of Daniel, Ezekiel and Ezra are foreign to Judaism; but they are related to the Zarathustran religion which was practised in the environs of these prophets during the Babylonian captivity. We shall return to this later. Let us keep in mind that we must identify the Son of Man of these prophets with neither the Messiah expected by Judaism, nor — from our perspective — with Christ.

Enoch

The most fertile source of imagery of the Son of Man in this stream of Judaism is the *Book of Enoch* which is omitted even from the canon apocryphal books of the Old Testament. It is of a different kind than the three books cited earlier. Enoch, seventh in the series of generations after Adam, the grandfather of Noah, is not represented as the author of this book, he is the subject of it, although he himself also appears as speaker in it. He is the great teacher and initiate who has trodden the path into the spiritual world to its greatest heights and who can lead others on this path. The name Enoch means 'initiate.' Rudolf Otto believes that he may have been a 'master and saint of a particular religious conventicle;' Oscar Cullmann talks of 'esoteric circles of Judaism,' in which this book figured. There it must have been used as a kind of initiation text book. The fact that it was given the name Enoch may be connected with a tradition that can still be found in the legends of the Jews.* Enoch is already singled out in a telling manner in Genesis 5:24:

> Because God was pleased with Enoch he took him [into the spiritual world] and he was not found any more [in the earthly world].

* M.J. bin Gorion, *Sagen der Juden,* I, p.290. See also Emil Bock, *Genesis,* p.63ff.

This event is described more vividly in the legends of the Jews:

> And the Lord took Enoch to heaven in a storm, like Elijah the seer.

There we find the following explanation:

> But the light of the highest soul, that which fled from Adam, rose up again and was preserved in a treasury until the time when Adam's children themselves had children, and when Enoch was to come. Then this highest light of the holy soul entered into Enoch, and Enoch attained the same greatness that had been Adam's before the Fall.

According to this legend it was not when Adam died that a part of his soul was taken away and preserved in 'pristine' condition, but when he saw 'that he was naked.' We shall see that this concept is the key to the whole *Book of Enoch* and its naming.

In his careful investigation, Rudolf Otto has shown that the *Book of Enoch* is permeated with Iranian-Zarathustran elements which are foreign to Judaism. The divine names 'Great Saint,' 'Lord of Spirits,' 'Aged Head,' 'Ancient Head;' the basic theme of the fight of the forces of darkness against the good angels, the role of the various classes of 'spirits' and the heavenly archetypal human being, (Gayomart): all point to this origin. Irrespective to which epoch the two versions (Slavic or Ethiopian) of the *Book of Enoch* still extant may belong, it is unmistakable that this book has 'come out of the living stimulus of two religious worlds coming into contact with one another'

(R. Otto). We already know when this contact took place: during the Babylonian captivity.

The inadequacy of scientific research conducted to date into this well-known connection, is that it restricts itself to the plane of literary investigation. In the context of current attitudes to scientific study it can hardly be otherwise. Consequently, the question of the reality of spiritual worlds, supersensory prophetic experiences or spiritual beings altogether, is not even raised. But if one deals only with the literary reflection of such realities, is that not to be like a person who, looking at photographs, is interested only in the clothes people are wearing, or their hairstyles, or even the type of paper and the developing agent used, rather than who actually is in the photograph?

We cannot be satisfied with establishing that the influence of Zarathustran-Iranian documents can be traced in the texts we are considering here, rather we must ask: what is the *spiritual* origin of the Daniel-Ezekiel-Ezra-Enoch stream? The Son of Man visions must have occurred. From where comes the affinity of these visions? Does it come from a spiritual being who became perceptible to prophetic seeing at the time of the Babylonian captivity? Was there in the environs of those prophets a spiritual influence, perhaps that of an initiate, that could awaken these perceptions? Then the choice of words and the terms used to describe what had been seen may have been influenced by religious ideas or teachings current in the other, the Persian people. But that is of secondary importance.

From the capacious *Book of Enoch* we can here only select what is directly related to our subject. As a more specific description of the being of the Son of Man we find, like the corresponding passage in the Fourth Book of Ezra, the following:

> [He was] kept by the Lord of Spirits (40:5).
>
> For from the beginning the Son of Man was hidden, and the Most High preserved him in the presence of his might, and revealed him to the elect (62:7).

In all four of the books which we have selected as our source, inspiring beings join the visions of the Son of Man and instruct the seers about the contents of their visions. It is also such inspirators who, in the books of Ezra and Enoch, relate the pre-history of the Son of Man. He is, then, a being who was kept hidden in the spiritual world until his time has come. But to the chosen ones he was revealed already while in his concealment; such revelations are described by Daniel and Ezekiel. The nature of the Son of Man is further defined by his perfect sinlessness:

> This is the Son of Man who has righteousness, with dwells righteousness ... his lot has the pre-eminence before the Lord of Spirits in uprightness for ever (46:3).

These two points: being without sin and being kept hidden, bring to mind the Jewish legend of the preservation of Adam's soul which did not become implicated in the sinfulness of Adam. That the Son of Man of the gospels also is beyond the curse of sin, and therefore above the Law, we saw in Chapter 2 (page 35).

As a being who, in comparison with humans and also with the various 'spirits' of the *Book of Enoch,* is 'super-individual,' the Son of Man is characterized by his deed of 'preserving the lot of the righteous' (48:7); indeed,

> in him dwells the spirit of those who have
> fallen asleep in righteousness (49:3).

'That can only mean: their spirit enters him in order to be preserved for the end' (Rudolf Otto). In the gospels and in Ezekiel we found that the Son of Man can duplicate himself, as it were, that his rank can be transferred to individual people. Here, with Enoch, he appears as the opposite, a collective being, in whom the spirits of the just are kept safe. The indwelling is mutual and reminds us of Christ's words:

> Abide in me and I in you (John 15:4).

It has the character of a 'Son of Man' saying, even though it is spoken in the first person.

But the Son of Man also appears in the *Book of Enoch* in the sense already known to us, in his collective character: Enoch is addressed as Son of Man by the angel who accompanies him, (60:10) in anticipation, as it were, of the honour that will be bestowed upon him thereafter in a solemn scene.

> And it came to pass after this that his name
> during his lifetime was raised aloft to that Son
> of Man and to the Lord of Spirits from among
> those who dwell on the earth. And he was
> raised aloft on the chariots of the spirit and his
> name vanished among them. (70:1f).

The word 'name' in the *Book of Enoch* refers to a higher member of the human being, corresponding approximately to the 'higher ego' in Anthroposophy. This term is used in the same sense in the New Testament, where 'names' are mentioned which are written in heaven (Luke

10:20) or in the Book of Life (Phil.4:3). In the sentence quoted it is assumed that Enoch already was in possession of his 'name' as an earthly being, and therefore was worthy of his special destiny.

The Legend of the Untarnished Soul of Adam relates that the 'highest light of the holy soul of Adam' entered into Enoch. The *Book of Enoch* describes in pictures how this happened until, finally, he is addressed by the Aged One:

> You are the Son of Man who is born to righteousness (70:14).

The *Book of Enoch* bears his name with full justification.

About the future of the Son of Man this book says:

> And the Lord of Spirits placed the Elect One on the throne of glory. And he shall judge all the works of the holy above in the heaven (61:8).
>
> And the sum of judgment was given unto the Son of Man, and he caused the sinners to pass away and be destroyed from off the face of the earth, and those who have led the world astray (69:27).
>
> The Elect One [Son of Man] shall begin to dwell with the elect (61:4).
>
> The righteous and elect shall be saved on that day ... and they eat with the Son of Man (62:13f).

The eschatology of the Son of Man is the same as in the gospels. Here as well as there we find the sitting on the throne of glory and the last judgment. There is also a corresponding image in the New Testament to the image of eating with the Son of Man. Matthew records the words of Christ spoken at the Last Supper:

> From now on I will no longer drink of this gift of the vine until the day when I, in renewed form, drink it with you in the realm of my Father (26:29).

An earlier promise to his disciples says:

> You shall eat and drink at my table in this kingdom that I bring (Luke 22:30).

Here too, then, there is the image of a heavenly meal as a symbol for the future union with Christ. These words have been handed down in the first person, but they are among the disclosures of Christ and have their counterpart in the Son of Man teachings of the prophets.

The typical difference between Enoch's Son of Man figure and that of the gospels is that Enoch has none of the prophesies concerning Passion, death and Resurrection. The Son of Man is not expected on earth and consequently the Passion announcements are missing. It was therefore difficult for members of those esoteric circles in which the *Book of Enoch* was influential, to grasp the idea that in Christ the Son of Man was incarnated. But this is also what Christ expresses with the words:

> Do not put your efforts into acquiring the perishable nourishment, but the nourishment which endures and leads to imperishable life. The Son of Man will give it to you (John 6:27).

Future perspectives

Here Christ, too, links the images of feeding to the being of the Son of Man. The Son of Man of the *Book of Enoch* could also still have spoken this sentence, had he ever appeared as a speaking person. But he never speaks. He is spoken *about.* A characteristic difference. Enoch's Son of Man does not have the degree of presence that speaking represents. There he is beheld from afar, and those who speak indicate him across the distance. In keeping with this, the image of feeding is also placed in the far-off distance. But through Christ the Son of Man himself speaks:

> Yes, I tell you: If you do not eat the earthly body of the Son of Man and drink his blood, you have no life in you. Whoever eats my body and drinks my blood has life beyond the cycles of time, and I give him the power of resurrection at the end of time. (John 6:53f).

This sequence of statements confirms that the body and blood of the Son of Man are also the body and blood of Christ. The Son of Man is incarnated, is present in Christ. And so the meal of eternal life does not remain a spiritual image of an event in the beyond, it becomes reality in the Eucharist.

If one were to assume that the image of the Son of Man from the *Book of Enoch* was familiar to some of the disciples, that would be another specific reason why they could not grasp the words about the flesh of the Son of Man (John 6:53ff), indeed, why they left him (6:66). From John's account it emerges that it was not the actual twelve disciples who turned away from him for this reason (6:67). It seems all the more possible that we are dealing with as it were 'orthodox' members of an esoteric group for whom the *Book of Enoch* was crucial. Christ replied to their doubts with the words:

> Do you take offence at this? What will you say when you see the Son of Man ascending again to where he was before? (6:61f).

For Enoch believers that would mean: Christ is indeed the pre-existing being whom they know, and who, after his return to heaven, shall be the judge of the last days. But they now also have to grasp that, contrary to their expectation, he is now living in a physical body. At any rate, it is striking that Christ instructs them, using an argument from Enoch's esoteric wisdom and referring to the Son of Man.

Let us go back once more to a passage of the *Book of Enoch* (62:7) which was mentioned earlier (page 75). There it says that the Son of Man had been hidden by the Most High *in the presence of his might,* but that he had been revealed to the elect already during the time of his seclusion. According to the *Book of Enoch,* power is bestowed upon the Son of Man only in the final days, when he sits on the throne of his glory and dispenses justice. Before that, he is known only by the saints who have died and become one with him, and the chosen ones among human beings on earth. There is a parallel in the attitude of the Christ. We have seen (page 17) that he reveals himself to the disciples as Son of Man and commands them to be silent until the Son of Man has risen from the dead (Matt.17:9; Mark 9:9). So he conforms to the rule of the *Book of Enoch:* he reveals himself only to the elect — before his coming into power, meaning here, for as long as his self-chosen powerlessness shall last. And that lasts until his death on the cross. With the Resurrection he comes into his own kingdom and his heavenly power. 'Before his power' the disciples have to keep his secret.

Last Judgment

As judge of the final days, the Son of Man in the *Book of Enoch* does not have mild features. His judgment is of Old Testament severity. Matthew, the most Jewish of the gospel writers, portrays the Son of Man on the Day of Judgment with just as severe aspect. There, after the sheep had been separated from the goats, the Son of Man speaks:

> And they will become subject to the aeon of anguish, whereas those devoted to God shall find the aeon of life (Matt.25:46).

During his life on earth the Son of Man is full of gentleness, love and compassion. He consorts with tax-collectors and sinners and tries to save what is lost. These human traits must be absent in Enoch's Son of Man who does not become human and does not get to know human feelings. He cannot appear as a helping brother to human beings.

Just the same, Enoch, like the gospels, does also show a more intimate relationship than the legal one that normally exists between judge and judged. Of the sinners the *Book of Enoch* says:

> After that their face shall be filled ... with shame before that Son of Man (63:11).

Before a judge one is conscious of one's guilt. But one is ashamed before someone whom one wishes — but has failed — to emulate. Shame before the Son of Man means that he represents a standard which, as human being, one ought to measure up to. A similar relationship, remaining in the human sphere, between the Son of Man and the souls comes to expression in the words of Christ, recorded by Luke:

> So be of wakeful spirit at all times, school your souls in prayer, so that you may become strong to live through all that is coming without being harmed, and be able to stand before the revelation of the Son of Man (21:36).

One becomes worthy to stand before someone by striving to attain his rank. This is not the attitude assumed before a judge, rather that inspired by an ideal. The affinity of the Son of Man with all human beings comes to expression by the fact that one can be ashamed before him, or can strive for worthiness to stand before him. It is difficult to imagine that Christ would have said: become worthy to stand before *me*. That could only drive us to either despair or arrogance. We cannot measure up to him in worthiness.

In the *Book of Enoch,* as well as in the gospels, there are images of a function of the Son of Man which go beyond the end of the aeon and the Last Judgment. In the *Book of Enoch* (45:3f) 'the Lord of Spirits' speaks:

> On that day mine Elect One [the Son of Man] on the throne of glory ... and their [the elect's] places of rest shall be innumerable ... Then will I cause mine Elect One to dwell among them.

The 'Elect One' is another name for the Son of Man who, like the name itself, is transferred to the redeemed human spirits. The parable of the 'innumerable places of rest' evokes the picture of a large building — which actually appears elsewhere in the *Book of Enoch.* After the destruction of the earth

> the Righteous and Elect One shall cause the house of his congregation to appear (53:6).

Thereby the mission of the Son of Man reaches into the next aeon. Another passage says:

> He proclaims unto thee peace in the name of the world to come ... all shall walk in his ways ... with him will be their dwelling-places, and with him their heritage, and they shall not be separated from him for ever and ever and ever (71:16).

The redeemed part of humanity passes into the future world with the Son of Man.

This imagery is akin to the words of Christ in a prophecy recorded by John:

> In Father's house there are dwellings; otherwise I would not have said to you: I go there to prepare a place for you. And when I go to prepare a place for you I will come to you anew, and I will take you to myself so that where I am you may be also (John 14:2f).

The difference between the sayings in the *Book of Enoch* and those of John's account is again determined by the fact that Enoch's Son of Man remains a wholly celestial being, whereas the gospel's Son of Man speaks of the incarnated Son of Man. He 'will go' (return again) to where Enoch's Son of Man has remained. He will 'prepare the place'; Enoch's Son of Man waits until the elect, 'walking his ways,' come to him. There is more authority and vigour in the words of Christ. However, it must be borne in mind that the passage quoted above from the *Book of Enoch* (71:16) was spoken after the human personality Enoch had been elevated to Son of Man status, so that both figures — the Son of Man as heavenly being and the human being Enoch — merge with one another. Enoch himself, although not himself a redeemer figure, is nevertheless a Son of Man initiate who has gone ahead and awaits his disciples at the destination, the end of his paths.

Christ's words, although they are in the first person, nevertheless correspond to the images and words used in the language of the *Book of Enoch.* In so far as theologians accept as genuine those words of Christ which have their equivalent in the *Book of Enoch,* they conclude that the Christ must have known the *Book of Enoch* and from time to time used its pictorial language. It is not only possible but very likely that Christ Jesus came into contact with the esoteric circles centring on the *Book of Enoch.* But when he uses images and words from this book it is certainly not because they are in the book and pleased him, but because he knows that the being who in this book is called the Son of Man, is contained within himself.

4. The Son of Man in Anthroposophy

We are now going to look in Rudolf Steiner's Anthroposophy for an answer to the question of who the Son of Man is, and I must ask readers who are not conversant with Anthroposophy to listen with an open mind to statements that may appear incredible — yet perhaps no more incredible than is the Son of Man wisdom of the Jewish tradition, or of the gospels themselves. Most of us nowadays are quite prepared to accept as mythology a good deal from old documents, which does not raise questions of truth. At best, what is written in the gospels raises the question of faith. But it is foreign to the spiritual life of the twentieth century to acknowledge these same things as a objects of cognition. All the more fortunate are those who can overcome the prejudices of present-day scientific and popular thinking and find contents in the old religious documents confirmed by modern spiritual research. It would take us far beyond the scope of this book to explain from the fundamentals the anthroposophical concepts which we shall make use of here. Readers unfamiliar with Anthroposophy may find references to the relevant lectures by Rudolf Steiner helpful in acquiring the necessary basics. Those who do not want to go to that trouble are asked to treat what will be described in the same spirit in which they approached previous chapters. They will then come to see parts of an edifice of knowledge that, in splendour and richness surpasses by far the pictorial world of, say, the *Book of Enoch,* and is moreover built on a solid foundation of cognition.

The story of Adam and Eve is regarded as a myth nowadays. Anthroposophical research has revealed that, although it is told in mythical pictures, it is based on historical fact. Adam means simply: human being. (We have already noted that the Hebrew word for Son of Man is *ben-adam.)* The names Adam and Eve are collective designates for that group of humanity who lived before the 'Fall' and were ultimately caught up in this event. Although these names also apply to a single human couple that stood out among its fellow humans and can be regarded as representatives of this early humanity, we are at the moment dealing with the general meaning of these names.

The souls of human beings are formed out of an all-encompassing soul-like substance, just as the physical bodies are built up out of the general substance of earth.* This soul shared by all humanity rested upon that particular group of people. This is why it is also called 'Adam soul.' In order to avoid a total catastrophe through the Fall, the spiritual leadership of humanity retained a part of the substance of this 'Adam soul' in the spiritual world; thus it did not enter the sinful part of humanity's history. One can envisage the process of division more readily by assuming that this Adam soul consisted of large reserves of soul-forces which at that time had not yet been used up in the forming of individual souls. Bearing in mind, also, that supersensory 'substances'

* With regard to this indication and the following quotations, see Rudolf Steiner, *Christ and the Spiritual World,* (Lecture 3), and *Pre-Earthly Deeds of Christ.*

never are neutral substances in the physical sense, but have the character of beings, one finds it easier to conceive that the particular part of the 'Adam soul' which had been retained itself took on the nature of a being. We came across this superhuman being in the last chapter, in the legend of Adam's Untarnished Soul. And the Son of Man in the *Book of Enoch* is a being without sin, preserved by the 'Most High' in heaven. It is obvious that in the Jewish legend, in the *Book of Enoch* and in the statements of Rudolf Steiner we are dealing with one and the same being.

Pre-earthly deeds of Christ

Anthroposophy has more to say about this being than is contained in Jewish wisdom. Three times he was mediator of the deeds of the pre-existing Christ in epochs called Lemurian and Atlantic periods. As sensitive organ, feeling for the suffering of earthly humanity, he became aware of the dangers humanity was exposed to through the Luciferic influence. 'He sought in his inner being fully to feel this tragic aspect of humanity's development.' In Chapter 2 (page 60) we saw how Christ describes the Son of Man as a soul-being who extends his perception into all human souls, who perceives when 'one of the least of my brothers' is given food or drink, is clothed or, conversely, is ignored (Matt.25:35ff). That is a characteristic of the Son of Man which he evidently keeps for all time. He already has proved it when he assisted in the three deeds of the pre-existent Christ. From his parting from the earthly path of fallen humanity to the Last Judgment, this quality characterizes his role in the development of humanity.

This quality should not be thought of as limitless

dedication only. Rather, the case is that the soul-processes of all human beings are reflected in the collective Adam soul-being, as if they were its own. This relates the Adam soul (or, as we said, the Son of Man) to Christ, who has the same relationship to the 'I' of human beings as this soul has to the soul-nature of all human individualities. Thereby it was enabled 'to be penetrated in the spiritual world by the Christ being.' Christ entered into the Adam soul, 'ensouled' himself in it, as later he 'embodied' himself in Jesus, and through this union he was able to heal the soul-forces of earthly humanity. The Christ being evidently needed a mediator between his divine nature and the supersensory members of human beings, a 'transformer,' in order to impart his forces to humanity. The Adam soul is neither divine nor human, but an intermediary being, suitable for this function.

Of the consequences of these three deeds of Christ mediated by the Adam soul, we shall refer to three that can also be traced in the *Book of Enoch.* Because of the influence of the adversary powers, Lucifer and Ahriman, human beings had become so pressured and bombarded by their sense-impressions that no contemplation, no controlled inner life could arise. Through the first of those deeds of the Adam soul together with Christ, this overwrought life of the senses was toned down, so that *wisdom* could enter the souls. In the *Book of Enoch* this mission of the Adam soul is reflected in a characteristic of the Son of Man which appears repeatedly:

> In him dwells the spirit of wisdom (49:3).
>
> All the thirsty ... were filled with wisdom, and their dwellings were with the righteous and holy and elect (48:1).

> His [the Son of Man's] mouth shall pour forth all the secrets of wisdom and counsel (51:3).

Before being returned to humanity by the Son of Man, the destiny of wisdom is described in a way that makes it appear as a spiritual being:

> Wisdom found no place where she might dwell. Then a dwelling-place was assigned her in the heavens. Wisdom went forth to make her dwelling among the children of men, and found no dwelling-place. Wisdom returned to her place and took her seat among the angels (42:1f).

This image shows that there once was an archetypal wisdom which was lost in the time before the Son of Man imparted it again to earthly humanity.

For the second deed accomplished by the cosmic Christ together with the Adam soul, the latter had to travel from planet to planet in order to counteract the influences which, activated by Ahriman and Lucifer, caused disorder in vital human organs.

> The third post-Atlantean cultural period we call the Egyptian-Chaldean, came into being partly through the fact that souls still experienced the effect generated by the sun-spirit [the Christ] as he ensouled the being [of the Adam soul] ... during its circuit of the planets. This resulted in that science of planetary effects which we have before us in Chaldean astrology.*

* Rudolf Steiner, *Christ and the Spiritual World,* lecture 3.

In the *Book of Enoch* chapters 41 and 43 are headed 'Astronomical Secrets,' and the third part of this work is called the 'Astronomical Book.' It is a part of Enoch's elevation to Son of Man status that he is led through all the heavens by the Archangel Michael.

> And he showed me all the secrets of the ends of the heaven, and all the chambers of all the stars, and all the luminaries (71:4).

On his way to acquiring his status as Son of Man, Enoch takes the same road as the Adam soul had taken on the occasion of that second cosmic event.

One of the consequences of this second event was the proper development of human language. Larynx, tongue and throat had become decadent, and healing these organs was a first step towards enabling language to rise above simple exclamations as the expression of the inner state of the body. It became able to 'grasp objective concepts' which, in turn, led to the human word which serves the life of the spirit. Thus the Adam soul is also the mediator of word power. This is reflected in the *Book of Enoch:*

> And the *word* of that Son of Man shall go forth and be strong before the Lord of Spirits (69:29).

The third deed of the cosmic Christ, clothed in the Adam soul, concerns the human soul organs. They had been thrown into confusion by the Luciferic-Ahrimanic beings.

> That which would have created chaos and disorder in the human soul had to be conquered; it had to be expelled ... [This battle] is mirrored

> ... not only in Greek mythologies, but also in the mythology of the most varied peoples ... The memory of it is contained in all the images which, as St George conquering the dragon, have left their mark on human cultures.*

The Son of Man chapter in the *Book of Enoch* is completely dominated by the battle of the good angels against the wicked spirits. As such are named Leviathan and Behemot (60:7), who correspond to Lucifer and Ahriman. Michael repeatedly appears on the side of the good angels, although not so much as fighter but as proclaimer of the judgment coming to the wicked angels (67:12).

Supersensory members of the human being

The *Book of Enoch* either goes back to ancient wisdom that knew of this multifarious being, or it had its origin in visions and inspirations which imparted this pictorial knowledge. The Son of Man being is unmistakably identified by his origin, his pre-history, his nature and his mission. The reflections of those three cosmic deeds are even recognizable in detail. Not as clear, but still recognizable, is the relationship of this Son of Man to Christ. The two components of that complex being, who comes into existence three times, are not differentiated. This leads to the initially confusing situation that in the *Book of Enoch* the Son of Man is also called 'my son' by 'the Lord' (105:2) on one occasion, and is thereby raised to the rank of a divinity. In Chapter 2 we saw that in the gospels the Son of Man never appears as Son of God.

Lack of knowledge of the nature of human, let alone superhuman, hierarchical beings, has also coarsened and falsified the image of Christ. We cannot properly deal with the subject of our investigation unless we acquire some basic knowledge in this field. We human beings are earthly beings only as regards our body. Already the forces of growth and life (the etheric body) belong to another sphere. Our soul (the astral body) has its own independent origin in a second sphere above the world of matter, in the soul-world. And our actual spirit being, our 'I,' is spirit of the world-spirit. Only during our life on earth are these four members of our being at our disposal. In the hour of death we first discard the lowest of these members, three days later our life forces merge into the ocean of etheric forces of the world. At the end of the after-death events which are called purgatory or kamaloka, our soul organism, too, lets go of earthly things and dissolves into the world from which it has come. At the zenith of our life after death we are purely spiritual beings who only retain as much of our discarded bodies as is left over of plants in the shape of seeds when they die in winter.

All hierarchical beings above us, being invisible, have no material (physical) body. But, depending on their rank, neither do they have the other sheaths or 'bodies' which constitute human beings. Thus, the angels still have an etheric organism, the archangels a soul organism as their 'lowest' member, and the Mights do not have even this any more. Their lowest member corresponds to our 'I.' On the other hand, these hierarchical beings have some members 'above' the 'I' which we humans will only be able to develop in aeons to come.

In thinking about Christ it would be presumptuous of

* Rudolf Steiner, *Christ and the Spiritual World,* lecture 3.

us to try to conjecture which of the divine 'members' of his being might correspond to our soul and perceive our love for him. But what we are able to know on the strength of Anthroposophy, we may also apply: it is a distortion to sentimentalize the image of Christ by endowing it with qualities of ordinary human feelings. In reality, it is not a loss when the image of Christ is again elevated to the plane of the divine. It elicits deeper feelings of reverence, of devotion and of gratitude, better able to bridge the gap between our souls and the divinity of Christ. Only now do we grasp the magnitude of the sacrifice and offering of self that Christ had to make when becoming human.

Being 'ensouled' in the Son of Man was already a sacrifice for him; we described this earlier. A soul which sensed and reacted in an earthly-human way was not fitting for one of his stature. In order to empathize with humanity, he had need of the union with the Son of Man. The ability to feel with humanity was the particular characteristic of this soul-being (page 87). It is, of course, true that Christ is love in his essential being; after all, his sacrifice came about because of this love. Only, we have to imagine this divine love as being far superior to human emotions and feelings. It was a new experience for him to become aware of the ways of the human soul. This awareness was mediated to him by the Son of Man.

The Adam-soul

In Rudolf Steiner's above-mentioned lecture, *Pre-Earthly Deeds of Christ,* there is a statement concerning the Adam soul, the Son of Man, that solves a mystery we have encountered more than once. Ezekiel speaks of the being that appeared to him from above (page 68). For this seer, the remarkable thing about his vision was that a being like a *human* should appear in the higher world. And for Daniel and Ezra, too, the similarity to a human being presented by the Son of Man must have been the characteristic feature of this being. The *Book of Enoch* emphasizes that the face of the being beheld there 'was the countenance of a human being' (46:1). Now, from the lecture mentioned we learn that the Adam soul (that is, the Son of Man) 'would have had the form of an angel,' had it not been changed by the indwelling of Christ. Imbued by Christ, it took on 'etheric *human* form.' Material, earthly bodies like the one Christ was to assume later, we see with our physical eyes. Etheric figures are beheld in the etheric realm; and we have seen (pages 63) that the visions of Daniel and Ezra occur as they are raised up to the etheric realm. The Son of Man could be perceived there, supersensibly, because he had assumed an etheric form; and he was seen in the image of a human being because this form was a human one. This should remove any last doubts that the figure beheld by Ezekiel really was the Son of Man, even if it is simply called 'man.'

Having an etheric body was even further from Christ's own nature than having an astral body (a soul). But this, too, happened; the Adam soul, united with Christ, took on 'etheric human form' and thus added a third principle to the being created from Christ spirit and Adam soul, namely an etheric organism. This etheric body received its human form through Christ, who is himself the archetype *(eikōn)* of the human being, whom he created in his own image. An etheric body could only conjoin with the soul-being of the Son of Man. We must therefore imagine that before Christ assumed a physical body he was a supersensory God-Man, consisting of the God 'I,' the Adam soul and an etheric body shaped like a human. The Adam soul and this etheric body united with the Jesus child of Luke's Gospel already at his birth, the Christ 'I' with the thirty-year-old Jesus only at the Baptism in the Jordan.

The two genealogical lineages attributed to Jesus by Matthew and Luke respectively, made David Friedrich Strauss doubt their historical validity. The fact that two different places, Bethlehem and Nazareth, are mentioned as the residence of Jesus' parents, is one more reason for contemporary theologians to regard the stories surrounding the birth of Jesus as mythology. Rudolf Steiner solved this riddle, too, by recognizing that there were two Jesus boys, each with his own genealogy, whose parents had, prior to their birth, lived in different places. One of these boys came from the lineage of Nathan. He is the subject of Luke's Gospel. This boy did not have an ordinary human 'I,' that is to say, he was not the incarnation of a human being. He had a 'provisional I,' a member of his being that 'acted as an I.' One must not imagine this 'provisional I' to be some kind of stop-gap that is not quite durable or solid. The literal meaning of 'provisional' is 'forward-looking.' That is exactly what is meant here. This 'provisional I' looked ahead to the point in time when the Christ 'I' would incarnate in Jesus of Nazareth. And when it is said that this provisional 'I' 'acted as an I,' it does not mean that it was less than a human 'I;' but it does mean that it was not a *human* 'I' (see Appendix 1).

This member of his being, given to the Jesus boy of Luke's Gospel was the pure Adam soul, retained in the spiritual world since the Fall; in other words, the Son of Man. It was not a single human individuality that lived in this boy, but the archetypal soul of humanity, *the* human being, the 'new Adam,' 'the second human being from heaven,' in contrast to the first Adam or — as Paul calls him (1Cor.15:45) — *ho eschatos Adam,* the last Adam. However, this last expression ought really to be translated or paraphrased as 'the eschatological Adam,' the Adam who will be there at the end, who is active from now on until the end of the earth, just as the first Adam set his stamp on humanity from the beginning. Paul did not use the designation Son of Man. But it is clearly discernible that he knew of this being and recognized him in Christ. Paul, too, believed in keeping knowledge of the Son of Man within esoteric circles, as was done with the *Book of Enoch* and later also by Christ, as we have seen.

In the other Jesus boy, he of Solomon's lineage and of whom Matthew speaks, there lived, reborn, a great human individuality, namely Zarathustra. This great spirit left the body of Jesus in his twelfth year and transferred, as 'I,' to the other boy. The 'twelve year old Jesus in the Temple' was now a uniquely constituted being: he had the pure Adam soul within him as a 'provisional I.' Into this soul there now entered the real human 'I' of one of the greatest leaders of humanity, the 'I' of Zarathustra. Thus came into being the abundance of wisdom of the twelve-year-old Jesus who now lived with this make-up of his being until the Baptism in the Jordan.

Zarathustra

Who was Zarathustra? Historians can make little of the evidence from classical antiquity and ancient Persian sources. In one version he was born 600 BC (Porphyr), other sources (Plutarch, *De Iside et Osiride,* XLV) have him living around 6000 BC. Both are approximately right. According to Rudolf Steiner's spiritual-scientific investigation, the original Zarathustra was the founder of the Persian religion and worked around the time suggested by Plutarch. The next incarnation was again in the Persian-Iranian region. At that time, in the sixth century BC, he lived as Zaratas at the court of Persian kings. Pythagoras was his pupil there and, according to Rudolf Steiner's indications, he also became a teacher to the Jewish prophets in Babylon during the time of captivity of their people. This indication is confirmed historically by Muslim chroniclers who, however, give a different account of the teacher-pupil relationship. According to them, Zaratas was the pupil of the prophets Jeremiah and Ezra. Suffice it to say that there is testimony to the contemporaneity and to the relationship between Zaratas and the prophets of the Exile.

With that we have found the key to the Persian-Iranian influence evident in the books of Daniel, Ezekiel and Ezra and, at least in the sense of a tradition, also in the *Book of Enoch.* The core of these Zarathustran-Persian elements are the visions and the teachings concerning the Son of Man. So advanced an initiate as Zarathustra or Zaratas does not only impart knowledge. As spiritual leader he can also train his pupils in supersensory perception. Consequently we must grasp the thought that knowledge of the Son of Man was imparted to the prophets by

Zaratas. And that means: in the sixth century BC Zarathustra prepared the leaders of the people in whose midst he was to be born for the coming of the Adam-soul, the Son of Man. He laid the foundations for the coming of one (Luke's) Jesus boy, into whom he himself would enter from his body (that is, that of the other Jesus boy) in his twelfth year of life. Humanity was to look ahead to this being, too, as, by different paths, it was prepared for the coming of the Christ.

The most significant event in the earthly existence of the Son of Man is the Baptism in the Jordan, eighteen years after the Zarathustra individuality had entered into his being. He who walked towards his baptism was a being constituted of the body of Jesus, the Adam soul and the Zarathustra 'I.' At the Baptism Zarathustra left this being, and his place was taken by Christ. The Adam soul, the Son of Man, was permeated for the fourth time by Christ, the Son of God, this time on earth in a physical body. And, as we shall see later, this union remained. But the individuality whom we have to regard as the archetypal physical human being, the 'first Adam,' had incarnated in John the Baptist; he had lived through the whole history of humanity, incarnation after incarnation, and had also been incarnated as Elijah. Let us remember: Adam's original being had been split asunder in the Fall. His 'I' and a part of the shared soul of humankind continued to live on earth and became the progenitor of humanity. The other part of this complex soul-being had been taken from him and preserved in the spiritual world. Now Adam's 'sister soul'* again stood before him, the Adam 'I;' and this 'I,' having been resurrected in John the Baptist, had

* Rudolf Steiner, *The Bhagavad Gita and the Epistles of Paul,* lecture 5.

to facilitate, Christ's entry into his sister soul through his deed of Baptism.

Once before there had been a meeting between the Adam-John 'I' and the Adam soul when Mary, having conceived the child Jesus, went to visit her relative Elizabeth who was six months pregnant. The Adam soul began to prepare its body in Mary's womb. In Elizabeth's womb the body of John the Baptist was forming. When Mary stood before Elizabeth and greeted her, the child in Elizabeth's womb stirred. This occurrence, not uncommon in the sixth month of pregnancy, would hardly be mentioned in the gospel if the intention were not to hint at an unspoken mystery. Still more light falls on the subject from the context of our study: what had belonged together since primordial times met again at this moment. The Adam 'I' greeted the Adam soul physically in the only way possible for it under the circumstances.

Soul and body

For descendants of Adam the fate of the body was also the fate of the soul. Under the influence of Lucifer and Ahriman, bodies had become denser and more impenetrable, and so human consciousness of the spiritual world was increasingly obscured. From the way the physical body of John the Baptist is described in the gospels, we can deduce that owing to the strength of this mighty individuality and his ascetic exercises, his body had become so permeable, that John was able to perceive the approach of Christ to the earth. In this connection, the following words of Christ about John the Baptist become particularly clear:

> Among all who were born of earthly mothers, none is greater than John the Baptist. And yet the least of the beings in the heavenly world is greater than he. (Matt.11:11).

In other words: since the creation of the world no greater spirit has arisen from the succession of generations than John, but now a new humanity is beginning to emerge in the kingdom of God come to earth. The first example of a human bodily nature of this kind, that of Jesus, is imbued with the Adam soul and the Christ spirit. Founded by the second Adam, the beginning of a new humanity has been established, no longer by physical procreation but through the indwelling of the Son of Man and Christ in human souls. The following words of the Baptist can therefore also be understood in a more specific sense:

> After me comes he who was before me, for he is greater than I (John 1:15).

The Adam 'I' in John proclaims that Christ existed before him. If this sentence referred merely to the existence of the Baptist, it would be so self-evident as to be barely worth expressing. And another saying of the Baptist takes on a deeper meaning:

> He must increase, but I must decrease (John 3:30).

The time of the first Adam has come to an end; the time of the new, the second Adam, is beginning and will last to the end of the age.

The union of Christ with the *Adam soul* lasted during his life on earth, and it explains the riddle of the Son of

Man words which we studied in Chapter 2. It is also the reason for the interplay of the Son of Man discourses and the words in the first person which we looked at earlier. If the reader will peruse Chapter 2 again, it will be seen that from the full text of the gospels alone we discovered that for which we now have learnt the concrete basis.

The union of Christ with the *Son of Man* lasted beyond death and Resurrection. The first known appearance of Christ after his ascension, was experienced by Paul at Damascus. The Acts of the Apostles describes it as an experience on two levels:

> As he was on the way and came near to Damascus, suddenly a light from heaven shone around him. He fell to the ground and heard a voice (Acts 9:3f).

According to Rudolf Steiner's research, 'the light in which Christ clothed himself' was the Son of Man, because the Christ 'had taken him as his soul sheath through which he then continued to act.'* The voice that Paul heard we must regard as the voice of Christ; this means that the Son of Man *did* go with Christ through death and Resurrection as had been foretold. And they remained united during the continued working of Christ.

The manner in which Rudolf Steiner frequently described the appearance of the returning Christ as an etheric figure, leads one to surmise that this event could be similar in kind to the visions of the prophets, if not in the degree of its importance, then in the way in which it can be perceived, supersensibly. We have previously mentioned Rudolf Steiner's indication which points out

* Rudolf Steiner, *The Bhagavad Gita and the Epistles of Paul,* lecture 5.

the basis for the visions of the seers: when it became filled with the Christ spirit, the Adam soul took on etheric human form (page 63). Will it be united again with Christ at his Second Coming in the etheric realm and enable him to be perceptible? That would fulfil another of Christ's prophecies. On the one hand, he said:

> When I go to prepare a place for you, *I* will come to you anew and take you to myself ... I will not leave you as orphans. *I* shall come to you (John 14:3, 18).

That is how the Christ 'I' announced its Second Coming. But on the other hand, Christ also said:

> You will see the *Son of Man* ... in the ether-cloud realm of the heavens (Matt.26:64).

and repeated this statement several times (pages 49f). Both will happen: The Second Coming of the Son of Man as a vision in the shape of Christ, and the Second Coming of Christ, having become 'soul,' in the Son of Man.

The prophets Ezekiel and Daniel show the deity, 'the lord of lords,' as judge in temporal courts of law, sitting in judgment upon the enemies of the people of Israel and upon those who had broken away from him. In these prophetic visions the God of the Old Testament, Yahweh, can still be discerned in his relationship to the people of Israel. But the future transfer of authority *(exousia)* and glory *(doxa)* to the Son of Man is also already announced in Daniel 7:14 and 27, as is his dominion *(archē)* over all peoples of the earth. In the gospels and in the *Book of Enoch* the prophecies concerning the Son of Man extend to the Last Judgment of all humankind. We have seen (page 36) that, in contrast to the tribal gods, he embraces all humanity with his being. As we now know, his role is as formulated by Blumhardt:

> In an earthly court the judge judges. In the heavenly court he who is judged judges himself.

Or, in concepts developed in this study: The criterion for achieving the ultimate purpose of the world is the indwelling in human soul of the Son of Man, which, in turn, mediates the indwelling of the 'I' of Christ in the human 'I.'

> In him [the Son of Man] dwells the spirit of those who have fallen asleep in righteousness (*Enoch* 49:3).

Strangely enough, in the words of Rudolf Steiner previously quoted he does not use the term 'Son of Man,' although it is quite certain that that is who is meant. We shall now turn to those lectures in which the term 'Son of Man' is used in various ways. We shall show that in these passages we are dealing with the same being (or the same concept) which we have come across so far.

In the gospels and in the *Book of Enoch* we found that one attribute of the Son of Man is his ability to replicate himself, as it were, and to rise in human souls. In occult terminology, the expression 'Son of Man' is a technical term for various stages of development of human consciousness, more precisely for the prerequisites required for the development of the 'consciousness soul,' and also for the development of this 'consciousness soul' itself (see Appendix 2). In the relevant indications by Rudolf Steiner he describes the path of the human being to the Son of Man from the beginnings to its fulfilment.

Son of Man and consciousness soul

Anthroposophy posits three components of the human soul which have developed one after the other: The sentient soul in the Egyptian-Babylonian age which ended in the eighth century BC; the intellectual or mind soul which came into force in the subsequent Greco-Roman age; and the consciousness soul which is only about to develop in our cultural period that began around AD 1400. Sentient and mind souls are stimulated and receive their contents from impressions of the exterior world, which they absorb through feelings or assimilate through rational thought. With the development of the consciousness soul an important change takes place. The soul no longer relies for its secure foundation on the contents of the external world, but finds it in its own consciousness. Truth, for instance, no longer needs to be substantiated by external 'proof,' but speaks for itself through its spiritual quality. Only the consciousness soul has an alert organ for this. Consequently, spiritual truths become valid in the consciousness, even if they cannot be 'proved' in a conventional sense by means of reasoning. But that means that the consciousness soul can open to the spiritual world. The term 'Son of Man' for this constituent of the soul follows the pictorial meaning of the word, since the consciousness soul develops like a blossom from the existing stock of the human being, or — to use another picture — is born of him as a 'son.'

Son of Man and cosmic Christ

Rudolf Steiner gave the term Son of Man a second meaning when he spoke about the 'Sons of Man of past generations.' He says:

> Although in the fourth epoch normally only the mind soul was developed, there must, among the leaders of humanity, have been some who had already developed the inner potential of the consciousness soul, into which shines the spirit self. Outwardly, however, they would have looked like other people.*

Here the term Son of Man is used in the sense which we already know, and for persons we have also met before. Ezekiel and Daniel lived in the sixth century BC, Ezra in the fifth. The writer of the *Book of Enoch* must also be placed in the fourth post-Atlantean epoch, as must the 'Sons of Man of past generations' of whom Paul writes in his Letter to the Ephesians (page 60). We can now understand better how they came by their special mission. From the indication of time, that is, the fourth epoch (and no earlier) we can conclude, in addition, that one result of this investigation is correct, namely that Zaratas did indeed inaugurate the Son of Man stream (page 97).

The term Son of Man can describe three things: in a microcosmic sense, a stage of development in human consciousness; in a historical sense, leaders of humanity who have reached this level in advance of others, and in a macrocosmic sense that superhuman heavenly being

* *The Gospel of Matthew,* lecture 11.

whom we have come to know as the pure Adam soul. The first two meanings we have now also found in Anthroposophy. Concerning the third meaning, Rudolf Steiner makes the most tremendous statements about the Adam soul, surpassing everything we have heard so far.

In his lectures on the Gospel of St Mark Steiner draws a distinction between two cosmic beings in the Christ Jesus, namely, the cosmic Christ and the Son of Man. This is a natural consequence of the premise stated previously (page 94). In Jesus the pure Adam soul was incarnated. It had become the Jesus soul. When the Zarathustra 'I' left this soul again at the Jordan Baptism, the cosmic Christ 'I' entered it. Let us, for the moment, ask purely theoretically: what must remain, when Christ left this Jesus of Nazareth? Only the Adam soul, the Son of Man, would remain as a being separate from him. And that is how it is described:

> The chosen people had shown no understanding; whereupon the aura gradually withdrew from the man Jesus of Nazareth, and *Christ* and the *Son of Man*, Jesus of Nazareth, became ever more estranged from one another.*

From these indications we learn that Christ's cosmic aura could only maintain itself in the Son of Man, with Jesus of Nazareth as its centre, so long as a number of human souls on earth were available to serve as a substantial basis. Perhaps we may understand the 'dozen,' the 'twelvehood,' of disciples in this sense. Could if be that twelve representatives of the forces working out of the zodiac were required to keep the Christ aura secured in

* *The Gospel of Mark,* lecture 9.

the soul of Jesus — a soul which itself was not actually an ordinary individual soul? And might this aura only remain effective on earth so long as it had the 'houses' of the disciples' souls at its disposal, just as the sun sends its power to earth from the twelve heavenly 'houses'? Evidently, the conditions needed for the effective working of the Christ aura through the incarnated Son of Man were no longer met when the lack of understanding in the disciples came to the fore: in the betrayal of Judas, perhaps already in Peter's misunderstanding at Caesarea Philippi (page 15) and later in the disciples' flight in the Garden of Gethsemane and from Golgotha. It was not the Son of Man who was the cause of the estrangement between himself and Christ. Rather, he was the victim of this estrangement. This is how it might be understood:

> Everywhere, Christ is connected with a far-reaching, effective aura. This effective aura existed because he was linked in soul with the people he had chosen; and it existed *as long as* he was at one with them ...
>
> The people chosen had shown no understanding, and so the aura gradually withdrew from the man Jesus of Nazareth ...
>
> And whereas previously the cosmic Christ could act within the Temple and drive out the merchants, and could proclaim the most mighty teachings yet nothing adverse happened — now that there was only a much looser connection between Jesus of Nazareth and Christ, his enemies could prevail against him.

Christ was protected by the power of his divine aura. On occasion this shows, for instance when he is about to be captured. Then he slipped away 'through the midst of their ranks' (Luke 4:30, compare John 8:59). Human hands could not hold him. The Son of Man could only be caught and held when the Christ aura no longer worked in him in the way it had before. The gospel accounts of the Son of Man can be taken as literally as that. Earlier, we wondered why there is such striking emphasis in the foretellings of the Passion on phrases like: *the Son of Man* will fall into the hands of sinners, and similar formulations (page 34). We now have the complete explanation and confirmation; the naked youth who, according to Mark's Gospel (14:52), fled when Jesus was captured in the garden of Gethsemane was, according to Rudolf Steiner's investigations, Christ who, at this moment, freed himself a degree more from the Son of Man. This separation *had* to come if the capture — and the subsequent death of the Son of Man on the cross — was to become possible.

Golgotha: death of a man or a god?

There have been two kinds of misconceptions of the Crucifixion of Jesus Christ. One of these errors was promoted by a group of Gnostics in the form of docetism. This doctrine held that what hung on the cross was only the semblance of a body, so that no real, bodily death had occurred. This notion arose from the conviction that Christ, being of divine nature, could not have died like a human being. But since the event of Golgotha could not be doubted, they resorted to such explanations as: Christ's bodily nature had always been merely an illusion and no real human body; or else: Simon of Cyrene was crucified instead of Christ. This means that the real significance of the Crucifixion had been disregarded, for it is not fulfilled without the death of a human body belonging fully to Jesus Christ.

Church doctrine veered away from the whole truth in the other direction. It lost sight, too much, of the divinity of Christ. The Christ figure moved closer and closer towards Jesus of Nazareth and his body, until they were completely identical. The question which the Gnostics had wrestled with was not experienced any longer: how can a divine being die — how is this to be understood? Thus there arose and remained a concept of the death on the cross which hardly differed any more from that of ordinary human dying.

The death on Golgotha was a real death, and it was a death in a human body. But he who suffered this death was no human individuality: neither the Son of Man nor Christ can be described as that. There are many indications by Rudolf Steiner to the effect that Christ became more and more 'human' during the three years from the Baptism to Golgotha, even to the extent of experiencing fear in the garden of Gethsemane and ultimately suffering a very real death. Especially this last has had the most profound effect on Christian piety. For human feelings, the suffering and dying Christ was intimately near. He had become a brother to human beings. But the mystery of the Son of Man remained hidden, and with it the special circumstance only through which the suffering and death of a God even became possible. There were no concepts with which to grasp this death on the cross, because suffered by a God, was a cosmic event; and why, therefore, *this* human death was something unique in the history of the world.

And so, for contemporary humanity the question

remained: how can this death of a single individual have redeeming significance for human beings in all ages? We have very good reason, then, to concern ourselves with the mystery of the death on the cross.

Was it necessary for the bond between Christ and the Son of Man to loosen, in order that the death on the cross be made possible? Can we even imagine that Jesus Christ could fall ill during the three years between the Baptism and Golgotha? Is that conceivable of a being who was able to say of himself: I am the life? What would have happened at the Crucifixion if Christ had continued to be fully united with the Son of Man? Even the idea is unthinkable. But let it stand for a moment, for the sake of clarification. The Jesus body, nailed to the cross, would have been unable to die. The Crucifixion would have become endless agony. A further 'non-thought': perhaps the might of Christ would have been able also to blot out the mental component of the physical agony. Then there would have been even less possibility of death occurring. But it had to be suffered.

What was crucified was the real human body of Jesus of Nazareth. The Son of Man suffered death in a way which was akin to human experience. But Christ had to withdraw the cosmic power of his aura from the Son of Man if that death was to occur which he, Christ, wanted to experience. Only the Son of Man, released from the power of Christ's aura, could impart this experience to Christ. The fact that this release had taken place is the explanation for the otherwise puzzling words spoken by the sufferer on the cross: 'My God, my God, why have you forsaken me?' It is hardly for us human beings to try and decide whether this call was directed towards Christ who had withdrawn the essence of his divine power from the Son of Man, or if it was meant for the highest God to whom the intimate connection no longer existed which had been formed through the indwelling of the Son of God. If Christ was to experience fully the earthly death of a human being, then he also had to experience the abyss, which, in death, we must first overcome.

Again, it would be presumptuous of us to try and speculate how Christ experienced his death on the cross. It is certain, however, that it would be wrong to think of this experience in purely human terms. Earlier, when Christ's three deeds prior to his incarnation were described, we saw that the Son of Man had the mission to convey to the Christ 'I' the suffering of humanity which pierced his soul (page 87). So perhaps we may be permitted to think that the soul-being 'Son of Man' was able also to make accessible to Christ the experience of earthly suffering and death. In any event, the withdrawal of the divine aura of power from the Son of Man should not be understood to mean that Christ ceased to have a part in experiencing the destiny of the Son of Man. Christ suffered the full bitterness of death. But he could not have gone through this experience had he not taken on body in Jesus of Nazareth, or had he not had the mediating help of the Son of Man. He died in a body and a soul to which he had a different relationship than we human beings have to our body and soul. Nor had the complete immersion of Christ in the body of Jesus cancelled out the dissimilarity. Yet the power that emanated from the cross was a consequence of this dissimilarity.

The revelations of Anthroposophy convey nothing contrary to the predictions of Christ himself: the Son of Man was indeed tortured, crucified and buried.

The Son of Man as archetype

Besides mediating the experience of death, this being also had a second mission. For this, too, we find at least the suggestion of an answer in the cycle of lectures that have already given us so much information. There the image is described of the Son of Man as he stood, again bereft of the Christ aura, before his judges:

> Here before mankind ... there stood the human being with the *form* which the divine-spiritual powers had bestowed upon Man ... but ennobled, spiritualized by Christ's sojourn for three years in Jesus of Nazareth.*

And beholding him, the people should have said to themselves:

> That is my highest ideal standing there — it is the *form* I am to become through the most intense striving of which my soul is capable.

These sentences do not refer to a purified soul. Nor would that make sense as regards the already pure Adam soul that had become the Jesus soul. What is under discussion is a restored *form*, in other words, the bodily nature. *That* had been purified through the indwelling of Christ for three years. But Christ dwelt in it, clothed in the Adam soul. Was it this soul that had to transfer the 'impulse of the cosmic Christ' to the sheaths, to the etheric and the physical body of the man Jesus? Let us remember that on the occasion of the three healing deeds in the Lemurian and Atlantean period, the Adam soul took

* *The Gospel of Mark,* lecture 10.

on 'etheric human form' through the indwelling of the Christ spirit (page 94). In this form it had still appeared to the prophets at the time of the Babylonian Captivity, which implies that it had preserved this form through millennia, or had assumed it again in the sixth century. Since neither Christ nor the Son of Man had etheric bodies of their own, we have to assume that an 'etheric human form,' an etheric body, had formed from out of the general etheric world around the spiritual being of Christ as he united with the astral being, the 'Son of Man.' Irrespective of whether this assumption is true or false, the fact remains that the Son of Man clothed himself in etheric form even then. It is not specified whether the Son of Man took this etheric human form with him into the physical human body of Jesus. But if the incarnation of the soul-being 'Son of Man,' happened in the usual way of human souls, then he would have fashioned his etheric body in a manner appropriate to his soul. For how else could this etheric body of the Jesus child of Luke's Gospel have been formed? Be that as it may, it is very clear that the Son of Man has a tendency to form an 'etheric human figure' that conforms to his own condition, untouched as that is by Luciferic-Ahrimanic temptation. And now we can say: for this the Son of Man had been prepared and preordained — to sustain a first human form, wholly purified with the aid of Christ, through death and to carry it forward to 'bodily' resurrection.

Inner spiritual development, leading to unity of faith and knowledge, would not by itself have made brought human beings to perfection. In addition, something had to be transferred to them of the abundance of Christ's being, something of what had permeated the formative forces which shape the human body. Paul expresses it like this:

'the life that is awakened in the spirit-body.' (1Cor.15:44). What the apostle proclaimed was that the power which enabled the body of Jesus Christ to rise from the dead can be transferred to the bodies of human beings. Christ's abundance of being took on form in the body of the Son of Man. It was this bodily nature, worked on by Christ for the span of three years, which rose from the dead.

Luke's Gospel has a brief statement about the twelve-year-old boy Jesus:

> And Jesus progressed in wisdom, in maturity *(hēlikia)* and in grace in the sight of God and men (2:52).*

From his twelfth to his thirtieth year, it was the Son of Man who developed the *hēlikia* in the body of Jesus until, after the Baptism, Christ took on this 'stature.' The *hēlikia* is the bodily nature of Christ in which he resurrected. It is the 'spirit-body' that can also rise again in the human being. We can become Sons of Man.

Healing the bodily nature

Throughout the history of Christianity the resurrection of the body has been the great mystery. It became a dogmatic assertion that was increasingly incomprehensible, and so the view became widely accepted that Christian religious life is purely concerned with the soul and has nothing to do with the body. Thus 'resurrection of the flesh' was postponed to the last days; it had to be 'be-

* The word *hēlikia* also appears elsewhere in the New Testament, for instance: 'Which of you can increase his stature *(hēlikia)* by so much as a cubit, however much he worries?' (Luke 12:25). Clearly, reference here is to those growth-forces which bring about the form and structure of the body.

lieved,' as far as possible. But as the centuries went by it became increasingly clear that human bodies no longer provide a consciousness that makes supersensory perception or real faith possible. Although it is not true that our consciousness and our thoughts are products of our body, yet we do need our brain as a mirror for our consciousness, just as a mirror needs a backing of quicksilver in order that pictures can appear. A hardened brain can bring only the physical world into consciousness; it can no longer grasp thoughts concerning the spiritual world. The Fall has also affected our consciousness. In this sense, the overcoming of sinfulness depends on healing of the body. Something had to be done for the bodily nature of humankind before night set in irrevocably. The Mystery of Golgotha, death on the cross and the Resurrection, was accomplished for the benefit of the human body. Not only for a resurrection body at the Last Judgment, but already for the bodies of human beings living on earth. The emphasis moves to this truth when we have found insight into the mission of the Son of Man in the Mystery of Golgotha. Death had to be overcome where the power-base of death is: in the human body.

Christ and the Son of Man

It would be a tragedy if, through this insight, our faith in Christ and the image we hold of him were to be upset or diminished. The image of the Son of Man *had* to be separated in the mind from the image of Christ in order to make the distinction clear. That this has not happened before has been the cause of much confusion and has left many mysteries unsolved. Correctly understood, the result of this study can only be that the figure of Christ is freed of the all-too-human attributes with which it has been burdened, and can be raised again to its divine majesty. The fact that a mediating being, halfway between the Christ spirit and the Jesus body, was necessary allows us only now to see how long the road was to the incarnation of Christ, how great the divine sacrifice. The fact that this mediating being, the Son of Man, from the beginning of time had been prepared by Christ to receive him and enable him to become man on earth — this at last gives us a glimpse of Christ's divine working in the worlds of spirit before he came to earth; and of his sacrificial deeds *prior* to the last one in the Holy Land. Only in this way does the image of Christ once more assume the full dimension of a God.

By himself, the Son of Man would have been powerless. What he did in previous earth epochs were Christ deeds. What he did in the Holy Land and will do again until the end of time, are Christ workings. The Son of Man was and is an *instrument.* And if, having absorbed this book, one were to say again: Christ *is* the Son of Man, then this sentence would be ever richer in content. Only then is it correct. The 'I' of the Son of Man is Christ, in the same sense as the human 'I' is that spirit-being in our soul which alone enables us to be human. And therefore: 'The Christ Jesus suffered under Pontius Pilate the death on the cross ... Then he overcame death after three days' (from the Creed).

Appendix

1. The Adam soul

In the lecture cycle *The Bhagavad Gita and The Epistles of St Paul,* Rudolf Steiner says that this Adam soul has been incarnated *once,* namely in Krishna in ancient Indian times. Rudolf Steiner calls this great teacher of ancient India 'the highest ideal of humaneness, the perfection of humanity,' because 'the proto-human being, a genuine superhuman entity,' lived in him. Krishna was 'the best teacher for the human "I".' In this guise, then, the Adam soul appeared as educator of the human race towards its archetypal image. Rudolf Otto* has shown that the description in the *Book of Enoch* of the 'path of the soul upward' corresponds to the 'Indian theistic dogmatics of later times which, however, go back to old traditions.' If we again look at this fact, not from a literary but from a realistic point of view, we would have to say: the Son of Man who reveals himself to 'Enoch' brings with him the heritage of his incarnation in ancient India.

This information tacitly fills a frequently experienced gap in the notions about the various phases in the existence of the Adam soul. The descriptions and the names of this being vary in Rudolf Steiner's lectures. The reason for this is that special conditions prevailed here for which no available designation is adequate. Although this being

* *Reich Gottes und Menschensohn,* p.168.

without a doubt was of soul (astral) substance, an individualization occurred nevertheless, although not in the sense of a human 'I.' Perhaps one can assume that it came about through Christ's repeated indwelling on the occasion of the three Christ events in the spiritual world. As Rudolf Steiner describes the incarnation of this Adam soul in Krishna as 'the perfection of humanity,' as 'highest ideal of humanity,' it is unthinkable that, at that time, it was not constituted in a way which would correspond to the human 'I.' This becomes even clearer when it is called 'the best teacher for the human "I".' It could not have taught anything that was outside its own nature.

2. The Son of Man in Rudolf Steiner's lectures

In Rudolf Steiner's lectures there are a number of statements on the subject Son of Man which are not easily reduced to a common denominator. Depending on the context, this designation is used in various ways to describe different stages of the development of consciousness. For readers who want to come to terms with these variants, we shall now try to reconcile the apparent contradictions.

In the lectures on the Gospel of St John one can read:

> The 'Son of Man' is the 'I' and the astral body as they are born out of the physical and the etheric bodies in the course of the evolution of the earth.*

* *The Gospel of St John,* (Hamburg 1908), lecture 6.

Here we find the name 'Son of Man' used in a considerably wider sense, as a technical term of 'occult language.' The prerequisite for the spiritual development of each individual to the 'Son of Man' stage (as understood in this treatise) is the entry of the human being's spirit-soul substance into its body sheaths. Inasmuch as these sheaths were developed earlier (in the Saturn and Sun conditions of the earth), the 'I' and the astral body are 'born' out of them, so that, in the pictorial sense of the word which we met earlier (page 62), the relationship to the physical and etheric bodies is that of a 'son.' In the same occult language-usage the two sheaths that came into being first were called 'human being,' so that the term Son of Man (son of human being) is used in an exact pictorial sense. However, in the sense of the first three chapters of the present book, this term is here applied already to those parts of the human being which can, by rights, only be called the raw material or germinal substance for the 'Son of Man.'

We get nearer to the concepts formed in this study when we read in the same passage:

> This Son of Man who has detached himself from the womb of the Godhead, ... but in exchange acquires physical consciousness, is to be raised again to a state of divinity through the power of Christ ...

On entering the outer sheaths, astral body and 'I' are cut off from the worlds of soul and spirit. As we found in the main part of this book, only their elevation to a 'state of divinity' could give rise to a 'Son of Man.' We have to note that there existed a use of 'occult language' according to which they were described as such even before their elevation. This is no contradiction, rather an extended version of the concept.

In a sense similar to the passage quoted earlier, we find the concept Son of Man in the lectures *Background to the Gospel of St Mark.* In the sixth lecture, the kind of human consciousness which begins to develop at that point back in time to which our memory extends, is called Son of Man; the consciousness of the physical plane. It is contrasted with the dim but spiritual consciousness of the three first years of childhood out of which it develops; to which it is like a 'son.' In order to put this in line with our concepts so far, we would have to say again: the human consciousness from which the Son of Man is yet to arise in the human being, is here already given that name, referring to its *potential.* What is emphasized through this expanded use of language is this: The Son of Man is not 'inserted' into the human being from above, rather he comes into being out of the earthly human being from below, as it were; from the earthly, but ego-like consciousness.

In the lectures on the Apocalypse we find:

> When the human being becomes conscious of the soul-determined characteristics and the soul-determined human qualities of the astral world and the devachanic world (the land of spirits) [then a figure appears as a] clairvoyant vision [which is] also called Son of Man.*

This supersensory perception is described as a 'symbol of that which the initiate experiences during his initiation.'

* *The Apocalypse of St John,* lecture 2.

The Son of Man confronts the human being from outside, not yet as a being in the full sense of the word, but as a symbolic vision, a 'symbol.' The prerequisite for this is a perception of the 'soul-determined human qualities' of the astral and the spiritual world. The upper worlds have these qualities, since soul and spirit were formed from them and were then 'cut off.' During the separating process these qualities of the world of soul and spirit remain outside human consciousness. We have come to know that pure archetypal soul of humanity (that is, Son of Man) preserved in the spiritual world, as a being who has preserved in himself the 'soul-determined human qualities' of the world above, passing them on again to human souls; this is also what Rudolf Steiner means (see page 87). It may be regarded as the creative power that activates the consciousness of the 'soul-determined human qualities' of the upper worlds. And that would explain the 'clairvoyant vision' of the Son of Man at that stage of initiation.

In the lectures about the Gospel of Matthew, Rudolf Steiner says that at the time of Jesus Christ one could have said:

> Normally, so far, only the intellectual or mind soul is developed, which as yet cannot take in a spirit self; but from the same human being who now has developed the intellectual or mind soul as its highest member, the consciousness soul will develop as its child, its achievement; this consciousness soul can then open to the spirit self. And what human beings, in accordance with their whole nature, should develop as the fruit of their endeavour, as it were ... what was

> it called in the language of the old mysteries? It was called the 'Son of Man.'*

We live now in the age of the consciousness soul. Promoted by the experience of the catastrophes of our century it makes itself felt in an increasing number of people, and the substance of these remarks of Steiner's concern us therefore all the more immediately. We now learn more precisely than we could from the gospels or the books of the prophets, what the nature is of the microcosmic Son of Man, and how he comes into being. The consciousness soul, which can be developed as a maturing fruit of a human being capable of opening to the spirit self, makes us Sons of Man. That particular part of the soul which, going beyond an awareness of itself and of the world ('sentient soul') and beyond coping rationally with perceptions and events ('intellectual or mind soul') makes possible an objective consciousness of the spiritual human 'I' and of the spirit of the world — this soul member can open towards the first member of a human being, the 'spirit self' (manas), which belongs equally to human beings and to the spiritual world. 'Son of Man' is used again in the pictorial sense, as already described above (page 62): a being that arises out of the previous resources of a human being.

* *The Gospel of St Matthew*, lecture 11.

Bibliography

Cullmann, Oscar, *Die Christologie des Neuen Testaments,* Metz 1958.

Gorion, Micha Josef Bin, *Die Sagen der Juden I,* Frankfurt 1919.

Lietzmann, Hans, *Der Menschensohn,* Leipzig 1896.

Otto, Rudolf, *Reich Gottes und Menschensohn,* Munich 1934.

Steiner, Rudolf, *The Apocalypse of St John,* (Nürnberg 1908) London 1977.

——, *Background to the Gospel of St Mark,* (Berlin 1910/11) London 1968.

——, *The Bhagavad Gita and the Epistles of Paul,* (Cologne 1913) New York 1971.

——, *Christ and the Spiritual World,* (Leipzig 1913/14) London 1983.

——, *The Gospel of St John,* (Hamburg 1908) New York 1962.

——, *The Gospel of St Mark,* (Basel 1912) London 1977.

——, *The Gospel of St Matthew,* (Bern 1910) London 1965.

——, *Pre-Earthly Deeds of Christ,* (Pforzheim, 1913/14) Vancouver 1976.

Bock, Emil, *Genesis,* Edinburgh 1983.

——, *Kings and Prophets,* Edinburgh 1989.

——, *The Three Years,* Edinburgh 1995.

Index of biblical references